The Touch of Love

A Biography of Mildred Swan

Elsie Newman

PublishAmerica
Baltimore

First printing

ISBN: 1-4137-5502-X
PUBLISHED BY
PUBLISHAMERICA, LLLP.
www.publishamerica.com
Baltimore

Printed in the United States of America

Dedication

Swannie wrote the following appendage before her last illness when we were researching this biography together. I feel that there could not be a more fitting tribute to Swannie's memory than to start with her own words.

When I was about ten years of age a visiting aunt asked me what I wanted to do when I was grown up. Immediately I replied 'I want to be a missionary' although I did not even know at that time what the word really meant. I had heard it used many times by the pastor in the church our family attended and presumed it was something good. In my mind it always conjured up visions of saintly ladies toiling ceaselessly day and night in faraway places.

Later I changed my mind. I was not saintly and I certainly didn't envisage a future toiling night and day for anyone! In fact, while studying in Brighton Teacher Training College for a degree I imbibed certain ideas that would certainly have startled my God-fearing mother had she known, let alone qualify me for any Missionary College.

I was learning about evolution when people were forgetting that Darwin had put forward only the theory and not in any way a series of proven facts. I lost some years in this spiritual morass and when I eventually came back to my original belief in God was enjoying a college life of dancing, smoking, acting, flirting and trying to make myself very popular with my contemporaries.

But God had plans for me. I was brought face to face with the reality of spiritual life in remarkable way. Friends of mine were becoming rather concerned about my way of life and apparent disregard for all things religious. They arranged for me to a go on a camping holiday at a time when I was feeling particularly tired after a strenuous school term and very much in need of rest. But on arrival in Eastbourne I found, to my horror, that it was a

Christian camp. I was so annoyed that I nearly turned and left immediately. Inherent good manners and a certain grudging respect for my friends, who certainly cared for my welfare, made me stay. But it would be for only a week, not the planned fourteen days, and with it came the proviso that I need attend none of the evening meetings.

All went well for the first six days and I quite enjoyed myself. The bracing walks along the coast and nutritious meals were having the desired effect and at the end of the week I felt much healthier, but I was still determined to return home the next day. Good manners prevailed again and I decided that it was only right that I should attend at least one of the evening meetings. And in a wonderful and unexpected way God spoke to me. I spent the rest of that night on the rocks at Berry Head committing my future to God and promising that my life would be His and that I would serve Him wherever He wanted. He took me at my word!

Almost immediately on my return I applied for a place at what was then known as the Churchmen's Missionary Society in Bristol. After studying there for three years I was accepted at the end of the course for work in Morocco. That was in 1941 and Britain was in the middle of the Second World War. It was almost impossible for civilians to board a ship to take them anywhere and I was told to have patience and continue teaching until such time as I could sail. I was eager to be off and the wait was irksome, but I took another post as teacher and waited. It was 1944 before the telephone call came to say that I was to be in Belfast the following day to board the HMS Baltrover. This ship was part of a convoy of eighty ships carrying gold to Gibraltar and had spitfires flying above to protect the cargo. An auspicious start indeed for any young missionary!

Here I must close. This is just an introduction to myself and hopefully a tempting taste of that which is to come. After having written both prose and poetry over many years I must now leave the writing to another.

Mildred Swan
Kingsbridge, 1997

Prologue

WHEN MILDRED SWAN WENT OUT TO Morocco in 1944 it was only a week's journey by boat from Britain but, even then, it was as foreign and exotic as any country in the orient.

Leaving England during heavy bombardment in the Second World War, Swannie (as she was affectionately called) forsook the familiar country lanes and set the compass of her life towards Morocco. There she was to find her life's work among one of the Berber tribes, a nomadic people having no written language at the time.

The country had been a French protectorate since 1917 and well-planned towns with fine roads had been built. An irrigation project was also in hand and it was envisaged that by building great dams in the mountains large areas of desert could be turned into productive land. The French in no way interfered with the common Islam religion and all over Morocco could be heard the daily calls to prayer in the name of Mohammad.

There Swannie made her life; teaching, translating, radio broadcasting and generally caring for the Berber people in the Middle Atlas regions, reaching them by either donkey, bicycle, motorbike or jeep. She was a gifted and adventurous English woman who was convinced that God wanted her to work in Morocco and planned to go as soon as she had qualified from Missionary College. It was 1941 and the Second World War was at its peak so because of this Swannie had to wait three years for a ship to take her to Morocco, which proved very frustrating. But in 1944 a berth became available and she arrived in Morocco.

Over the years Swannie grew to love and respect the Berber people as she 'sat where they sat and ate what they ate.' Her first radio messages to the Berbers went on the air in the mid-sixties and years of hard translation work culminated in the production of the Gospel of John in the original Berber dialect twenty years later. Swannie wrote many books in the Berber tongue of Shilha and was also fond of writing poetry, which she had compiled later into a booklet with the help of a close friend.

When Swannie arrived in Morocco she stayed for a few nights in the 'white city' of Casablanca before going on to the mission station at Boujad, a fanatical Moslem city. It was there that she first came in touch with the Berber people and was able to get to know them better. Swannie's poetic words describe her own feelings for the Berbers: 'I see them always through a lover's eyes and approach them with the touch of love.'

Swannie later moved to a mission station at Demnate which was situated at the foot of the Middle Atlas. She was there in the midst of a Berber population and found them to be a strong, warlike and intelligent people who appreciated very much the trust of others if it were given. Their dignity was most attractive to Swannie; poor women and children keeping the same observance of accepted custom and good manners as carefully as members of any wealthy family.

At that time the majority of Berbers were still to be found in tents on the slopes of the Middle Atlas or on the plains outside the nearby cities. One day as Swannie struggled with language problems and feeling rather frustrated, she watched a line of little donkeys toiling along the dusty path skirting the mission house in Demnate. Each one slowly and wearily carried two large slabs of salt attached to their back and hanging down over each flank like a sandwich board. The donkeys were from a small village beyond which ran a little stream with pink oleander blossom beside it. They travelled slowly on through the green olive groves, past the wild vine and with all the loveliness of the distant blue hills stretched out before them. But Swannie was convinced that the little donkeys could see nothing except the dust rising beneath their feet as they staggered wearily along under the weight of their burden. Later she saw them returning down the same road but then they were merry and free, carrying no load, the heavy salt slabs having been lifted in the market place. The journey for them, she was sure, had now become a place of beauty, with pink oleanders, wild vine and olive groves and the beautiful hills rising up in the distance. Swannie took the illustration as an encouragement to herself and never forgot the message that the little salt donkeys symbolised. She might often become weary with the burden of learning, depressed at the magnitude of the task before her, but one day the load would lessen. Then she would be free to see the beauty of the people as she lived and talked freely among them.

The above example was typical of Swannie's approach to life and its difficulties. Perhaps one of the poems she wrote at that time would be an appropriate introduction to the story of a woman who offered her life to God and was given a deep love for the people she had gone out to Morocco to serve. It shows how much she utterly relied on God:

Guidance

You know what you are doing, Lord—I do not!
So keep me on the track
and say 'Just follow me';
I won't turn back.

You can see the journey's end—I can not!
So guide my feet along
and if I feel your hand
I won't go wrong.

Your purposes unfailing stand—mine fall!
So wean me from my own,
train me to hear and heed
your call alone.

Chapter 1
Introducing Swannie

MILDRED ROSA SWAN WAS ONE OF a family of six and always proud of her surname. She also knew it caused comments, sometimes not of the most complimentary kind, so she dubbed herself 'Swannie' and was always known by that name to friends and colleagues who used it with affection and the greatest respect. During her growing up years, Swannie's main delight was reading. She had a vivid imagination and one book she was particularly fond of was *At the Back of the North Wind* by George McDonald, a well-known children's writer who was a contemporary of C. S. Lewis.

Always fond of writing herself, she liked to explore into the minds of people and write about their different foibles, often wandering into the world of nature as she did so. She confessed with a little remorse and much amusement that the first poem she wrote about the family cat was one of which she was not proud. In fact she never dared to have it printed as she did so many of her others.

Although young people were not known officially as

'teenagers' in Swannie's day, she still had many of the worries associated with growing up. As well as the usual problems Swannie suffered with congestion of the lungs and was made to stay in bed for almost the whole month of February each year. She was a loner so sometimes quite enjoyed the quietness of those months because as soon as the fever began to ebb, she could read to her heart's content with no interruptions from the family. Mostly in those days her reading consisted of the English classics and she devoured with passion such authors as Dickens, Elliot, the Bronte sisters, Jane Austen and other well-known authors. It was obvious from an early age that Swannie was particularly gifted in languages and art, but also had an insatiable desire for any kind of learning. After much discussion and pleading on Swannie's part, her father eventually decided she could go on to do teacher training. He would pay for her continued education with one proviso: that she promised not to marry. Married women were not allowed in the teaching profession at that time and he had no intention of wasting good money on his daughter's career if it were to last for only a year or two. Swannie was delighted to agree; she desperately wanted to be a teacher and marriage did not even enter her thoughts as she glibly made the promise. So off Swannie went to start further education at a teacher training college in Brighton.

It was while at college that Swannie came to a large spiritual hurdle in her life in the form of Freud and psychology. She soon came to realise that not everyone held the same Christian beliefs as herself. Swannie's mother had ensured that each one of her six children went to chapel on Sunday morning and Sunday school in the afternoon; they also said their prayers every night. There had been one incident at school where the Bible had been questioned and Swannie, at the age of fourteen, was amazed.

'What nonsense,' she had said to her friend, 'everybody must believe in the Bible! But we'll see what Miss Taylor says—she always knows everything!'

When their favourite teacher confessed with some embarrassment that certain parts of the Bible were being questioned, Swannie could not believe her ears. She went home that day feeling as she had done at the age of seven when someone said there was no Santa Claus. She decided that the truth could only be found fairly if she went to the library and studied other books. But none of the books seemed to help; in fact, they only confused Swannie more, so she decided to dismiss the whole matter from her mind and succeeded until she reached college. Then the subject arose again and she was told that, according to Freud, God was just a projection of the mind to satisfy the instinct of self-preservation. Swannie had not heard that one before but came to the logical conclusion that until she could prove otherwise, she must keep her mind open to the concept. She was not at all convinced by the arguments given, even then, but her active mind insisted she try to find out the truth.

Despite the deep thinking Swannie was known as a prankster. Without the calming influences of home her keen sense of mischief was fast developing. The college was single sex, as were most educational institutes at that time, but the young ladies were of an age when male companionship was something greatly desired. Swannie was no exception. She was bright, beautiful and very used to the company of her three brothers. Brighton was a lively seaside town and when her young friends started to complain bitterly of the shame of walking along the promenade arm in arm with three or four other females, she had to confess to the same feeling.

'I feel plain...boring...as if no man would ever ask me out on a Sunday afternoon,' one of her friends lamented. 'And everyone stares at us!'

A little extreme? Not for a pretty nineteen-year-old reaching out to life and the excitement of meeting members of the opposite sex.

Swannie decided something must be done about the situation and wrote a letter straightaway to her brothers. By return she received a huge parcel. Next Sunday afternoon saw three extremely smart couples promenading along the seafront. The young men were handsome in cream flannels, smart striped blazers and college ties while the women hung onto their arms and tripped along daintily in their Sunday best dresses.

It was only a sudden fit of giggles that attracted the attention of a passing lecturer taking her lone Sunday stroll. She turned round for a second look. Surely it couldn't be? But it was—Swannie and two of the taller girls had donned her brothers' college gear and were walking arm in arm with their smaller companions, enjoying the afternoon sunshine but unable to contain their giggles at the unexpected sight of a lecturer passing by. Of course there was trouble…but the girls so much enjoyed it and when the time came round for the annual concert, they were up on the platform in the same gear lustily singing 'Swanee River.' Even the lecturers greatly applauded the act!

Swannie also grew fond of dancing. Not having done much in early years it became a great passion while at college. She had always loved dressing up and found that her mother was still delighted to help in the making of costumes for her daughter to wear in the many college dramatic productions. She would not have been so pleased had she known of Swannie's newfound love of smoking, even though she did use a cigarette holder to make it look more sophisticated.

When she had gained the necessary teaching qualifications, Swannie left college and took up a teaching post in Kent. There she stayed with an old friend who had watched the deterioration of Swannie's spiritual life with some concern. When summer arrived the friend suggested that, exhausted as she was after a difficult year of teaching, Swannie should take a holiday. Two friends of hers were running a camp in

Eastbourne and she suggested Swannie join them. As she was feeling tired and in need of a rest, it did not take much persuasion for Swannie to decide to go. She knew that Eastbourne was an interesting seaside town and well known for its bracing sea air. The idea of reviving walks along the cliff tops before she had to return to next year's heavy teaching schedule sounded tempting. Swannie did not know it, but that holiday was to change the whole pattern of her life.

Arriving at Eastbourne, she found that the camp was situated in a very beautiful school with ample grounds and good tennis courts. Feeling quite happy and relaxed, she entered the dining room for lunch, only to find to her dismay that there were singing a song of thanks for the coming meal. It was a Christian camp and Swannie was furious. How dare her friend!

Inherent good manners persuaded Swannie to stay but she vowed that it would only be for one week and not the proposed fortnight as planned.

For the first few days she kept to herself, resting, wandering up the cliffs at Beachy Head, swimming, reading, and very much enjoying the sunshine. She avoided as many of the women leaders from the camp as she could and went to none of the communal meetings. As she had always enjoyed her own company, Swannie found it a refreshing change from school and her lively pupils. She would take advantage of the summer weather while she was there but definitely go home at the end of the week.

Then a surprise meeting changed Swannie's plans. She was browsing through some poetry in a small bookshop in the town when she came across Francis Thompson's poem 'The Hound of Heaven.' She had been introduced to it many years before and it was one of her favourite poems. As she read, softly mouthing the words, 'I fled him down the nights and down the day, I fled him down the labyrinth ways of my own mind...' Swannie was suddenly startled by a tap on her shoulder.

It was one of the young women in charge of the camp who said impulsively: 'Oh, Mildred, you're reading "The Hound of Heaven"—it is so lovely, isn't it?'

To Swannie's amazement she went on to quote the rest of the poem.

This particular lady was known to be a good musician but Swannie had never thought her interested in poetry, and certainly not capable of quoting a classical poem with such ease.

They chatted together for a few minutes and before parting the young woman said quietly, 'Mildred, it has been good to talk to you. I know you are leaving tomorrow but will you come into the meeting tonight? My sister and I are singing a duet and I should love you to share it.'

To her own amazement Swannie agreed to go and that evening took a solitary seat at the back of the meeting hall so that she could make a quick exit if necessary. The two sisters, one contralto and the other soprano, sang an old hymn that Swannie had always liked. Despite herself she felt a lump rising in her throat as she heard the words they were singing.

'…You are the potter, I am the clay…'

The words stuck fast in Swannie's mind and suddenly she knew with a great certainty that she had been led to this camp for a purpose. God was speaking to her…she had not been forgotten during those years at college when she had felt so mixed up and pushed her beliefs to one side. She had been wrong and the clever college professors were wrong too. God was alive and the Bible was true. A sudden relief surged through her whole body.

After the meeting Swannie went up to the two sisters and told them of her feelings and their cool reaction surprised her. They were pleased, of course she could tell that, but the elder said quietly, 'If you are really going to make big changes in your life then it has to be thought through. It might have to be everything or nothing! Think about what you have just decided during the night and then come to us again in the morning.'

Swannie spent that night by herself on the lonely cliffs of Beachy Head. In the darkness she questioned herself, knowing that if she did make a decision for Christ it would indeed have to be 'everything' for her. There were things in her life that would have to change and Swannie knew that would be hard. She went through the things she knew were not good and would not fit in for her with a Christian life. It might be alright for others but there was a smoking habit that was bad, totally out of control and that she could ill afford. Then there was the play she was acting in at the moment with the Amateur Dramatic Society. *The Ghost Train* was proving very popular in the London theatres and Swannie was playing the part of a woman who was completely drunk on a railway station in the production. Just for the fun of it and to impress her colleagues, Swannie was drinking a great deal of alcohol before each practice. She was being very much influenced by the company she was keeping, and caring far too much for the opinions of others. The third thing that came to Swannie's mind was her dancing. She knew that it was not in any way wrong but dancing had grown into such a passion for her that it was almost taking over her life.

Swannie started to reassess her priorities and then out of her handbag she took a full packet of cigarettes and as a gesture of repentance flung it over the cliff top and into the dark water below. From that decision made one summer's night on Beachy Head Swannie's faith blossomed; it was the start of a new life for her.

Swannie was always a person of action and almost immediately on returning home, she applied for a place at what was then the British Churchmen's Missionary Society in Bristol. She was accepted and took a three-year course after which she was thrilled to be chosen for work with the society in Morocco.

By that time it was 1941 and Britain was in the middle of

the Second World War and it was impossible for civilians to travel anywhere by sea. Swannie was told to continue teaching as she had done before, be ready to go at any time but to have patience. She was eager to be off and Swannie knew that patience had never been one of her strongest virtues, but there was nothing else she could do but wait. While she waited she took a post at a school in the south of England and settled down to teaching again.

In 1944 the call came from the Church Missionary Society at last. There was a berth available for her and a colleague on a ship that carrying gold from Britain to Gibraltar. It was to sail from Belfast the following day. This was exciting news and Swannie reached Belfast to board the HMS *Baltrover* amidst the turmoil of war. Their ship was part of a convoy of eighty with spitfires flying above to protect them.

An auspicious start for any young missionary and the journey Swannie made in 1944 was the start of her real life's work. She was in Morocco, Corsica and then Malaga, Spain, for almost the whole of the next forty years. She grew to love the Berber tribe of North Africa and served them for the rest of her life. Her only desire was to help them and she did that through living among them, learning their language and translating Scriptures into it. After she came back to England, Swannie returned many times to Morocco to her Berber friends, the last visit being when she was well into her eighties. She died in Kingsbridge, Devon, at the age of 89.

The Touch of Love is in some ways more a short account of Mildred Swan's life as a missionary than a biography in that many personal details were left out at her own request. She wished the book only to be published in order to stir up interest and support for the Berber work in North Africa by the telling of her own story. Hers was a heroic life and no doubt this will be done, although Swannie often lamented the fact that she had not been able to achieve more during her time among the

Berber people. But she also knew that some are called to sow, others to reap, and took great comfort in the fact that the Good Book says:

Unless a grain of wheat falls into the ground and dies it remains only a single seed, but if it dies it produces many seeds.

Chapter 2
Waiting Time

SWANNIE HAD ALWAYS FOUND TEACHING A rewarding task and after college continued happily enough for the next eight years. She found many aspects of the children's lifestyles and behaviour 'interesting' to say the least. Her middle-class upbringing had certainly not prepared her for some of the situations she was called to face but these were certainly good experiences for when she finally settled in Morocco.

Swannie's first posting was one of the most bizarre. She was teaching at a primary school in a small village in the south of England where there were some extremely poor but very tough little pupils. One of them was a little girl of ten whose name was Amy Brookes. She never kept still for a minute and one particular day shifted from three different desks in all of twenty minutes. Though she tried hard to control her annoyance, Swannie found herself gradually losing patience. The last straw came when little Amy dug her fingers furiously into the back of the boy sitting at the desk in front and then cheerfully took an onion out of her pinafore pocket and started sucking it loudly. A smile lit up the little face as Amy's eyes met those of Swannie and she pushed the remaining bit of onion quickly into her mouth and sucked her wet fingers with obvious pleasure. A class of forty grinning children between the ages of eight and ten waited expectantly. What could be done to contain one charming little girl who was disrupting the whole class? Swannie had been at the school for a few weeks by then and was beginning to understand the children a little better. She looked around, reflectively seeking a solution and her eyes rested on the large wood-burner in the centre of the classroom. Suddenly she had the answer to the problem of Amy's aromatic wanderings. Around the burner was a large, iron fireguard to protect the children from the hot pipes running up to the ceiling when the weather was cold. But it was a warm, sunny day and the burner was not in use so Swannie quietly moved the fireguard from the centre to the side of the room against the wall and placed Amy inside. The little girl's arms and legs were free and there she stayed, imprisoned but quite happy in her elevated position for the rest of the day. Not a solution many parents would find acceptable these days but remarkably successful at that time.

The children's extremely deprived backgrounds were so different from her own that Swannie became acutely sensitive to their needs. She soon realised that there were many ways in which she could help them, and not all educational.

One little boy, Terence O'Sullivan, was even poorer than most and Swannie's heart went out to him in his ragged, hand-down clothes. Young Terence's father gambled heavily and, try as she might, there was never enough food for their mother to feed the family properly. New clothes for the children were an unattainable luxury and Swannie was quick to notice the embarrassment on the boy's face as he took his place in morning assembly. No one wanted to stand next to him because the shabby clothes he was wearing were smelly. So, as an act of defiance, he always behaved badly when he went into class and was continually in trouble.

19

Swannie decided she would try and help him. First she spoke to the boy's mother asking for permission to take Terence home to Dover for the weekend as he was recovering from a severe attack of bronchitis and she felt the fresh air would do him good. The harassed mother was only too glad to agree and to Terence's delight he was taken on his first-ever trip to the sea. While there they had a shopping spree and on Monday morning Terence arrived at school bright and shining clean in new clothes from top to toe.

'Very smart, Terence...very smart!' the headmaster commented and the little boy beamed with delight. A huge grin stayed on his face for the rest of the day.

But badly off as Terence was, Swannie was soon to find that there were others in even more distressing need. At least he had a home to go to and a place to sleep. Some of the children had no beds to sleep in. One little boy used to sit on the railway siding waiting for his father and brothers to start work so that he could go into the little caravan they called a home and have the next 'turn' in bed. After a few hours he would arrive at school late and promptly fall asleep with his head on the desk.

It was during her years at this particular school that Swannie first realised how privileged her own upbringing had been, and to care passionately for the poor. She developed a hate of the obvious injustice in the world that was to stay with her all her life. Swannie was to meet many different kinds of people in later life but she always said that her first teaching experiences in England had been the best because it had helped give her an insight and understanding of people whatever their social circumstances. As one American colleague of hers was to comment: 'Swannie would have been as equally at ease with royalty as she was in a hillside tent sharing a humble meal with the poorest of Berber families.'

After four years Swannie moved to another school in Kent. Her main subjects were English and art and there she was able to take up the post of art mistress with enthusiasm. She had always been imaginative and relished the task of teaching the children many different kinds of art such as opaque, material printing, designing and story illustrations. Later she was able to help the children put on an exhibition of their work in the town hall. This second school was quite a change from the first and she relished being able to wander in the woods and practice the violin, which she had been taught at school but had long neglected.

Swannie always had the feeling that she was being trained for something different, even in what she called her 'wilderness' years at college when God was far from her thoughts. She made many friends during her first teaching years and one of those, a fellow teacher to whom she became very close, asked her to marry him. But Swannie's mind was not on marriage or settling down. She rejected his offer but they remained close friends. She was always conscious of the promise she had made to her father that she would make teaching her life's work and had no intention of relinquishing her career.

But when Swannie returned to teaching in 1941 after being accepted for work in Morocco by the Church Missionary Society, it was difficult to concentrate on the tasks in hand. Each day she prayed that a call would come from the society to say they had found a berth for her on some ship that would take her to Morocco and she could begin what she knew was to be her life's work.

What should be the next step while she waited? Should she be still and wait or seek to gain more experience in the teaching world. She decided on the latter and applied for a job as headmistress of a school in London and was accepted for interview. Swannie was surprised but then started to ask herself what she would do if she were offered the post. It was certainly a step up in her chosen profession but was it the right thing to do? So her mind was working as she made her way to the interview.

To Swannie's amazement she was offered the position immediately and couldn't help but be delighted. She accepted at once persuading herself that God must evidently agree with her decision. Perhaps she was doing such a good job of teaching in England that she must stay there! It was only when she was sitting quietly on the train travelling home that an inner voice spoke and she realised that no one except herself had made the decision. It had been her own unconditional choice. And what if a berth became available and she was ordered to Morocco at short notice? She could not accept the post—she must write a letter there and then to the school apologising for the inconvenience she had caused and explaining her reasons for having to turn it down. Being only human, Swannie cried a little as she sealed the envelope and said goodbye to her promising career in England. Then she sat back, dried her tears and in her own decisive way began think about the future. Whenever the society called she would be ready and waiting but in the meantime she would go back to her old school routine and plod on as usual.

Towards the end of her years at Missionary Training College Swannie and a friend were advised to take a walking holiday around some of the villages in the south of England. It was to be a time of preparation for the mission field as well as a refreshing break so they set out with very limited resources and many instructions as to how to conduct themselves in a Christian and maidenly manner! Swannie had a great skill with words, a definite talent for drawing and a unique sense of humour. She drew little sketches of both herself and her friend to show ludicrous or amusing situations they managed to get into on their holiday journey. These coloured sketches made each page come alive and were her own particular hallmark, together with the diary she so faithfully produced each year. The drawings were impossible to publish but as Swannie's writing never fails to make an impact some of her diary comments on that particular trip are given below.

Easter 1941

Having been impressed by a private interview with tutors at the college on the virtues of maidenly sobriety, Swannie set off with her friend with tongue in cheek and the resolve 'not to disturb their countenances by unseemly mirth.' The first day they found 'a laughing stream with a rejoicing bird'—which carefree words show just how high their spirits were.

Saturday, 23 March
Good Friday service in the little church at Doulting yesterday. The sun was shining through the eastern window and the aisles were fragrant with daffodils. What Easter loveliness! Sketched part of the village and later suffered a little dampening in the rain. Not our spirits, of course, in fact we nearly forgot ourselves and laughed at the bedraggled sight we made. Both of us are on bikes and I had a puncture at Blandford. Decided to get 'digs' at the next village. Called at a house—soldiers billeted, dared the inn—soldiers there! A final plea at the petrol station and we were taken in, clothes dried and a friendly welcome. Remembered the flesh needed feeding if we were to continue harbouring the spirit so ordered proper tea and breakfast for the following morning.

Sunday, 24 March
Easter Sunday communion in Puddletown and the church was full of soldiers. We were glad to see them. Went on to a hostel, which was an old converted workhouse, at Cerne Abbas. Cerne was so named because when Augustine was tied to the tail of a cow and pelted with mud down the village street, he cried out with saintly patience 'Cerne Deum' (I see God).

Monday, 25 March
Did not get in supplies on Saturday and (of course!) bought nothing on Sunday so ate some porridge and departed from hostel rather hungry and thirsty. Found a little shop open and bought some biscuits and drank some wayside water. The wind was bitter over the moorland but we threw back our heads with the very joy

of the open road and laughed our indifference to the billowing storm clouds. Bought a loaf of bread and, having strengthened the 'inner man' tackled Bedminster Downs. Rock House gave us a great welcome and we spent the evening in an impromptu praise meeting with uproariously joyful and hearty singing, a slow pounding on the piano and indescribable squeaks on an indescribable fiddle—but what a praise meeting!

Tuesday, 26 March
We had early morning tea—what bad missionary training! Sent back to the college half of our luggage, deciding it was better to live like tramps without a change of clothing than break our backs. Cycled into Crewkerne to take a women's meeting. We both spoke and sang a duet. One woman said we certainly looked as though our faith brought us joy. Had tea with an elderly man called Mr. Cross who held the hand of his second wife as she poured out the tea. A few others were there and we all sang the Fisherman's Grace while Mr. Cross beat time with his knife.

Friday, 29 March
What a send-off!! The dear folk all came out to wish us God speed and we were supplied with food for the way and left full of fresh enthusiasm. Had a pot of tea in a café in Axminster, availing ourselves of the Ladies Room and doing a little washing! The hankies dried later on the handlebars. Sheltered from the rain in the church for three hours. Did some Bible Memory and warmed ourselves by the radiator. Filled our fountain pens at the Post Office and continued on our way.

Approached Honiton and had a lovely view of Dartmoor—purple and blue and somewhat forbidding. Passed through Ottery St. Mary to 'Melverley,' a well-kept homestead on a hill facing a wood. A courteous old gentleman greeted us and we found ourselves sole possessors of a three roomed establishment plus bathroom, all very clean but with stone floors and no mat.

Saturday, 30 March
Went through lovely tree-lined lanes, which are typically Devonshire. Heated some beans and had a kingly feast with a grander view than the king himself. Went on a round of calls to the water mill and the village general store; invited to tea with the village gossip and heard extraordinary things!

Sunday, 31 March
A wet, misty day, rather cold. Cheerless? Certainly not as we were not dependent on the weather for our gladness. Attended a little congregational church and heard a message on 'Go and tell...Peter.' Eggs on green peas for dinner and as the stone floors were cold we retired to the church again for warmth. Found a haystack in a farmyard and gave the farmer the privilege of sheltering us. Ate our last slice of bread. Two brothers, a viscount and a colonel, invited us to go and sing hymns and stay with them for supper. The niece was there and played the piano. Given cake for supper as well as bread and cheese and marvelled at God's provision.

Wednesday, 3 April
Set off for Exeter from Dawlish. Superb view of the distant rises of Dartmoor. Visited the cathedral, which always fascinates me—a never ceasing wonder how human minds ever carry out this detail. Saw Thomas Mostyn's picture of Gethsemane and all thoughts of cathedral beauty left me as I saw the face of Jesus. Could only look and look again and felt an ache in my heart that I could not run inside the picture and assure him that such travail had not been in vain. Turned into Dunsford for the evening—the hostel was a little wooded cabin along the banks of the Teign. Felt humbled before the sweet purity of the little wild daffodils nodding to the rhythm of the water. The waterfalls are so white—I thought of Revelation, 'He showed me a pure river of water, clear as crystal, proceeding out of the throne of God and of the Lamb.'

Experiences such as these taken from Swannie's diary took place throughout the whole month's working holiday. She and her friend arrived back at Bristol on Saturday, 20th April, bedraggled and almost shoeless. They were both filled with a great contentment and Swannie knew that the month had been invaluable in her training as a missionary. Behind the tomfoolery there had been a deep consciousness of privilege and the experiences of those weeks had strengthened her confidence in God so that she could say when she returned 'His love to me was wonderful.'

After this holiday she entered the waiting period of three years until, almost miraculously, berths became available for her and a colleague to travel to Morocco in February 1944, while England was still very much at war.

Chapter 3
On the Way at Last

SWANNIE SHIVERED, DRAWING THE CURLY BLACK
collar of her astrakhan coat closer round her neck as she sat up.
The warmth was comforting; a February night in England she
could cope with—the middle of the Atlantic was quite a
different matter. From the bunk above came the sound of gentle
but rhythmic breathing. Her travelling companion, a young
woman also assigned to work in Morocco, did not seem to be
having the same difficulty as herself in catching hold of sleep.

She closed her eyes. She was so tired and the last two days
had been frantically stressful but as she lay there in the
darkness all Swannie could see was the pale and worried face
of her mother. There had been apprehension in the well-loved
voice during that last telephone call and at the end Swannie had
caught the hastily stifled note of panic. Her beloved daughter
was leaving for a country so far away and she did not know
when they would meet again.

It was only just over twenty-four hours since she had made
that call to her mother. Two days before she had been teaching

her class as usual and had rushed off as soon as the bell rang because she was going to tea with her friend, Kathleen. They both looked forward to these visits when they could laugh and talk together over old times as they relaxed in each other's company. Swannie particularly appreciated the meal ready and waiting for her when she arrived. But that night things turned out to be different.

'An urgent message has come through for you from the Missionary Society—you have to be in Liverpool by tomorrow morning!' Kathleen gasped.

Swannie's mouth had fallen open. All she could think of in the moment of panic was that her one good winter coat, a curly black astrakhan, was at the cleaners. There was no way she could go to Morocco without it!

When her mind had cleared Swannie grasped the garbled instructions. She and her travelling companion were to meet up with Mr. and Mrs. Albert Fallaize, respected missionaries in Morocco for many years, at Liverpool Station. There they would travel with them to Belfast where berths had been booked for them on the *Baltrover*, one of a convoy of eighty military ships bound for Gibraltar.

Then had come the second wave of panic. How could everything be done in time? It was 1944 and Swannie had almost given up all hope of travelling to Morocco before the end of the war. What about her trunk, neatly packed and ready for further movement but still stored away in the bible college at Bristol? And what about the next day's appointments? She was scheduled to take a lecture entitled 'The Gospel in the Heavens' and had prepared thoroughly for it—how could she miss such an opportunity of sharing with others some of the mysteries of the constellation?

Sleepless on her bunk Swannie gave a silent chuckle. It looked as if God had much more in store for her than giving a lecture on the stars.

Her mind raced on…

Having completed her training at the Bristol School of Theology in 1941, Swannie had applied to the Church Missionary Society for work in North Africa and been accepted. Morocco had been particularly brought to her attention and she became increasingly convinced that was the area in which God wanted her to work. The only slight difficulty was World War Two! At that time it was at its zenith and travel to North Africa seemed impossible. The War Office had assured Swannie that every ship was needed for military manoeuvres.

The delay was hard to bear. Swannie was by nature impatient and the vital energy surging within her was telling her to get on with the job. Yet the way was blocked. Was she being taught yet another lesson in patience and trust?

Accepting it as such and having little money and bills to pay, she had started teaching again and it was 1944 before the call eventually came. Fully awake now as the memories surged, Swannie found herself giggling as she remembered the next turn of events.

A few hours after arriving home from school she had stood at the top of a hill above the city of Bath complete with suitcase and black astrakhan coat which had been hastily redeemed from the cleaners. The friend also travelling to Morocco had arrived an hour before and stood beside her with a similar suitcase. As they rushed down to the bus stop, they saw the bus disappearing in the distance and despair stepped in. They would never get the train to Liverpool now.

The two young women had looked at each other.

'We will have to hitch a lift!' Swannie said quietly.

Her friend nodded. They had just made a decision that was, for two properly brought-up young English ladies at that time, momentous. If they were to catch the midnight train to Liverpool that was only one thing they could do. Rushing to the roadside, they stood boldly facing oncoming traffic and the first vehicle to come in sight was a jeep full of U.S. soldiers.

The girls looked at each other with raised eyebrows and then hurriedly passed up their suitcases to cries of 'Come on, gals…show a leg…let's have you up here!' from the uniformed men. Swannie found herself sitting on the lap of a handsome young G.I. and looked across with a grin at her friend who was equally positioned. They reached the railway station in plenty of time and amidst much laughter.

Safely on the train they both decided that the journey had not been too bad at all—in fact, rather enjoyable! But they were very relieved to see Mr. and Mrs. Fallaize waiting to chaperone them on their journey to Morocco. The couple had been waiting patiently for them on the platform at Liverpool and they greeted each other with warm hugs. Swannie remembered giving an extra prayer of thanks when she saw the two large trunks standing beside the couple, daubed all over with two names in white paint. Being rather a meticulous young lady she did not relish the thought of arriving in a strange country with no fresh clothes as well as no books.

At Belfast Swannie was so tired she remembered only customs—officialdom—customs again and a great desire to lie down before eventually being able to collapse on the bunk in her cabin. Now she could not sleep for excitement. Morocco was almost in sight at last.

Swannie had kept a journal from an early age. The best way to convey to readers the excitement and danger of that first journey can best be done by taking extracts from her diary for that time. She writes with her usual gift of observation and wit.

February 3, 1944
We are not in an ordinary common cabin. As the only two single ladies we have been accorded a suite! So, although water oozes through the floor, the matting belies close inspection and the bathroom infuses a certain unfragrance, we cannot complain. Anchor was lifted at 5 p.m. and the dear old British flag went up in a dizzy frame of white seagulls. I never thought of seasickness

until the waiter brought in our dinner of steak and vegetables liberally covered in greasy gravy. Then I felt an urgent desire to be alone. Only a few stayed the course this first night. It is very disconcerting to find one's body organs synchronising with the boat's movements.

February 5

After a good breakfast we joined in the physical training exercises organised by the crew. Very glad to be wearing my plaid divided skirt though at home thought not quite acceptable by some. At nighttime we only remove our shoes and always wear a life jacket. A constant reminder of the danger we are in. Made the most of a good lunch because a storm is predicted. Purser told us cheerfully 'we begin six meals tomorrow—three down and three up!'

February 9

He was right…we had three days of seasickness best forgotten. About 200 plates smashed to the ground in the kitchen, furniture slid all over the cabin and our suitcases literally chased each other over the floor.

February 13

A few nights after the storm a warning sounded that a submarine was in the vicinity. Down went the depth charges and there was a great rolling of the ship. Men shouted to each other and there was a real sense of impending disaster. Then all was quiet. The next day another alert sounded as we were finishing supper and seven enemy planes appeared on the scene. It was peculiar to hear the fierce barking of our guns as the planes droned around and unreal to contemplate an immediate close acquaintance with the Atlantic! The Purser had his bag of documents ready—this was action stations and not a practice this time. We saw one plane come down in flames and then three others. We are unhurt—are we not on the king's business?'

Swannie was always confident of her calling and quite sure that the convoy of 80 ships would remain untouched by the enemy simply because of the presence of the four missionaries on board. During one particularly difficult time she was heard reassuring the longsuffering captain that his ship could not possibly go down—there was a special work for her to do in Morocco!

The next short entry in Swannie's diary comes after her view of Gibraltar.

17 February
In a blaze of sunlight the convoy streamed triumphantly into the Straits. No one was lost and the thrill of being part of that majestic convoy of eighty craft will stay with me forever. We have to leave the Baltrover but are to spend a week in Gibraltar before leaving Morocco on a French ship. Perhaps there will be opportunity for us to explore.

Gibraltar, with its brightly lit shops and tall Spanish houses, entranced Swannie. There were barrow-loads of lemons and oranges, which she had not tasted for some years. The only trouble was they had no money to buy anything. Their cash had all been taken away at customs so Swannie and her friend walked around the shops buying imaginary presents to take home; beautiful articles that they knew were long lost to their loved ones back in Britain. But she felt sad at the sight of the Spanish women, so sombre and hungry looking in their black shawls and quite unlike the pictures she had seen of them with black shiny hair and bright eyes.

To Swannie's delight a permit was given for the four of them to visit the Europa lighthouse with the captain and purser as the master of the lighthouse had been a table companion on the *Baltrover*. It was a lovely bright day, with a glorious view over the harbour and at night it was a sight such as she had never seen before. Blue beams blazed down from different levels of the rock to guide landing aircraft and thousands of little lights glimmered along the shore.

Good friends had been made on the *Baltrover* and Swannie was especially glad that twelve members of the crew had accepted New Testaments. It was hard to say goodbye, but it was only when the four missionaries boarded the French ship that they realised just how different things were going to be on this second stage of their journey.

The *Hogard* was a boat taking French refugees who were escaping through Spain to Casablanca. Suddenly a lump of dry brown bread and a cup of foul black coffee replaced the big breakfast on the *Baltrover*. This also constituted the evening meal, together with some embarrassing spaghetti. The boat was full to overflowing.

At 5 p.m. on Friday, 25 February, the *Hogard* landed at Casablanca. The Arabs were in the docks acting as porters and Swannie's first impression of them was of an extraordinary assortment of dirty rags. It was too late for the passengers to disembark as the customs office was closed, so another night had to be spent aboard. That night somebody stole Swannie's toilet requisites as they hung in a bag out of the cabin window, which was not an auspicious start to her life in Morocco but which certainly gave her a taste of things to come. Next morning the French refugees were the first to disembark, to loud cheers and music from the regimental band. Swannie wondered wryly if the angels in heaven had prepared some kind of welcome for the landing of the little missionary party!

At Casablanca it was time for Swannie and her friend to say goodbye to their dear chaperones, Mr. And Mrs. Fallaize. Often in years to come Swannie would wonder how they ever would have managed those first few days in Morocco without the love and care of the more experienced couple.

One last catastrophe happened in Casablanca. Swannie's suitcase, containing books and documents that were very important to her, could not be found. She was very upset and, after fighting French officialdom, searched among the precincts of the dock for four hours without any success. She returned with her friend to the headquarters where they were staying and mentioned the loss briefly to an American chaplain and two officers who were visiting. To her surprise, the following Thursday the chaplain appeared with the suitcase. Rescued again by an American. Swannie found herself hugging the startled cleric in the joy of answered prayer.

Chapter 4
First Years in Morocco

SWANNIE'S FIRST BASE FOR A SHORT time after arriving in Morocco was at Boujad, a fanatical Moslem city standing on a great stony plain.

She knew it would be a long, tiring journey on the bus from Casablanca and was particularly apprehensive. The restaurant where they had eaten meals before leaving had not been very pleasant and Swannie felt decidedly queasy that particular morning. Even in England she had not been able to make a journey of fifty miles without feeling sick—and that was in a decent bus and with no live chickens dangling in front of her eyes squawking their distress.

But Swannie's confidence in prayer was strengthened that day. For the first time in her life she felt no sickness as the hot, bumpy bus sped across the miles. The noise and smell from both animal and human cargo became more unpleasant as the hours wore on but she almost started to enjoy the journey. She began to take an interest in the scenery around. It was amazing; the miles and miles of sandy hills, with dark clumps of trees spattered about in patches like some kind of welcome oasis. The valleys were being cultivated for crops by robed figures working with oxen and old-fashioned implements. Donkeys were everywhere, and Swannie's heart ached as she saw them bearing burdens that seemed too heavy for their thin little legs to bear. Brilliantly coloured flowers looking amazingly like some of those she was familiar with in England grew by the wayside and she made a note to study the names of all the beautiful plants when she had learnt the language. But learning to speak to the people came first and she looked with special interest at the little brown-skinned children as they sat in the dust and waved at the passing bus.

It was such an interesting journey. They travelled for miles along a long, straight road, passing Arabs on their way to market with loaded donkeys and strings of camels. They rose at one point to undulating countryside, dry and barren with no trees and on through tiny villages dotted about spasmodically. Swannie was enthralled by it all, but especially delighted when the saw in the distance the city that was to be her home. She writes in her diary that the journey to Boujad was the start of her own private 'cultural revolution.'

Boujad swarmed with little Arab boys, brown-eyed and laughing, naughty little imps. Swannie was particularly entranced by the hairstyles of the little Berber boys who had one long pigtail at the side of their head, apparently so that Mohammed could catch them up into heaven more easily! She had been warned to take little notice of them at the moment as they would be a nuisance, but she longed to understand their language and be able to talk to them. Boujad was indeed a learning place for Swannie. She came to realise very soon that to invite confidence and yet retain dignity, call for respect and yet give no rebuff, could only be done with the help of the one who gave his life for these little ones.

Swannie's home for the next two years or so was to be at the mission house. It was a white, flat-roofed building surrounded by pepper trees and her room was at the top, facing away from the city. To the left of the main building was a little school where she longed to teach, but she knew that the immediate task before her was to learn to speak the Arabic language proficiently. As she met her fellow missionaries and settled in to the day-by-day grind of language study, Swannie wondered how long her stay would be in Boujad. As she watched the little boys playing a sort of football game outside her house with donkeys and camels sauntering lazily past, she had the feeling that it would not be long. She prayed for courage to face the unknown, always fearing that she was a coward and might let God down.

The first few months in Boujad were exciting but difficult and her first meal was a particular problem for Swannie. No cutlery was provided so she had to say goodbye to her usual fastidious feelings. The guests were all seated on a divan round a long, low table. A large table was placed in front of them on which a sort of solid-looking stew towered pyramid fashion on a bed of couscous, a white semolina dish that Swannie had not encountered before but which, she discovered later, was eaten at almost every meal. A little girl brought a bowl of warm water and then to Swannie's delight the hands of each person were washed. Then the right hand only was inserted into the bowl and a handful of couscous taken out and shaken into a ball that had to be snipped with the thumb into the mouth. It was difficult and Swannie found that, hard as she tried, she could not make her couscous into a ball and she was certain it would never reach her mouth. But as she had to choose between starving or taking an untidy handful, she chose the latter but had to confess in her diary that it gave her 'much temporary discomfort!'

Another eye opener for one with such a fastidious nature was Swannie's first visit to the market. What a scene met her eyes. Hundreds of Arabs sitting on mats in front of the weirdest assortment of wares. Patient little donkeys and crowds of unruly little children. A great crowd squatted round the Story Teller and Swannie soon realised that the stories he told were usually unclean. She longed to sit there beside him and talk about God's love. Often she wondered whether the precautions taken by the missionaries were necessary. Must they always work in the dark and would any Christian work ever be achieved except at the risk of open persecution? Swannie was much perplexed over the months concerning the attitude of conformity to both French and Arab requirements but as a young missionary she did not feel in any position to voice her doubts. But her young spirit longed for a band of fearless ones who would not count the cost of an open witness and she prayed for discernment between compromise and discretion. Swannie did not seek only a familiarity with the language, she sought an understanding of the Arab mind without which she felt there was no way to succeed in such a strange country.

It was six months before Swannie felt able to speak more than a few words in Arabic even to her colleagues and it was only a sudden emergency that eventually helped her gain confidence.

The country was still suffering the effects of war and the husband of the senior lady missionary at the station had left for chaplaincy in England. His wife was called to Casablanca with the other junior missionary and Swannie found herself in charge with just the hurried instruction to 'make them understand you can't speak the language.' There was no indication given of how she was supposed to do this with her limited vocabulary! She was able to speak a little French with one of the women helpers but at first she had panicked. Why, she knew nothing at all about this strange country and could speak only a few basic words and those stumblingly, how would she cope? Then she regained her courage. God had brought her to Morocco under the most unlikely circumstances so she must be strong and trust in Him.

Strange as it may seem to those who knew her, courage was

something Swannie always feared she lacked. She continued to pray for it over the years for only she knew the weakness of her own body and the despair she had so often felt in her younger years when confronted with danger of any kind.

So she struggled along with the few words she knew, giving a bright smile and using her hands to try and explain what she meant. To her surprise Swannie found that people were listening to her and really trying to understand. The children, especially, seemed able to know what she meant and before long there were three or four round-eyed little girls coming to visit her every day. Of course this was the chance Swannie had been waiting for and she learned to love them as they listened to her stories and talked excitedly to each other.

Then one day she met a little boy, a curly haired, lonely little boy crying at the gate of the city with his dead mother beside him. She had died of starvation. Swannie took him back to the mission station with her, fed him and cared for him. As he grew older he became more and more mischievous—a naughty little boy but so dear to her. His name was Hamid meaning 'little loved one,' and he certainly was that! It was through this little boy that Swannie learned to talk easily in the local dialect. Another one who helped her was the local fakeeh (native leader) who was a secret believer. It was lonely in the mission house on her own and she began to talk more easily with him.

When the missionary's wife left, Swannie was having lessons in Arabic with a well-educated man who later became a government minister. He was a Berber and it was during her lessons with him that Swannie's interest in, and love for, the Berber people developed. She met with this gentleman every day, having coffee with him after lessons and talking over the language and culture of the Berbers. When the missionary couple returned to Boujad, Swannie's language was much improved and she was more able to help with the daily activities of the mission station. One Easter Day they had a picnic and as she sat by a lovely river nearby and she thought back to a similar but yet very different Easter excursion spent with a friend in England at the end of a bible college term. Swannie had been praying for guidance then as to where her future missionary life would be and, as she dipped her feet in the cool refreshing water in the stream outside Boujad, she could only praise God for his guidance. Oleander bushes hung over the stream with their pink buds already opening and the banks were a riot of pale blue scabious. Bright sunny marigolds sat beside deep scarlet blood-drops and tall, fair mignonette and, special to Swannie, some pale love-in-a-mists that she felt she must have. Doubtless there are more exotic names for these flowers but in her diary she calls them all by the English names she had known at home.

They left the water's edge and trudged over the plains to visit the home of a water carrier. There they were met with wonderful hospitality. Mint tea was served and a million flies swarmed round them as they drank thirstily and ate little honey cakes. Then an old woman performed a spontaneous dance for them that Swannie thoroughly enjoyed but which the older missionary said was probably 'not very nice!' But as Swannie remarked, 'Where ignorance is bliss…'

Going further they met a dear little boy named Mustapha with his mother, a beautiful fair Arab who had another baby but was recently divorced by her husband. Again they drank mint tea and had fellowship with a thousand more flies!

Another incident in Swannie's early learning experiences was what she called a Special Day at the Boujad Mission Station.

The controller of the area and the local doctor were coming to dinner and there were such preparations at the mission station. There were lace mats and finger bowls and the missionary wife was in a state of panic. But things went terribly wrong and the tragedy was, in brief, the food. The first course was a violently bad concoction known only to the cook, the second course a bony old duck and the third course a peculiar mystery that didn't stand up as it should but slopped down helplessly all over the dish. The guests left early, obviously for the same reason that the missionaries were glad to see them go. They tried hot peppermint and camphor pills but all covered quite a distance that night walking to and fro.

Swannie's next move was now on the horizon and to her delight she found it was to be to Demnate, a mission station situated inland at the foot of the Middle Atlas Mountains and consequently very near to the Berber tribes.

Before she was to move Swannie was able to take a break at a place called Bene Mellah, a lovely, white-walled town at the foot of the Atlas Mountains. The hills rose up behind, ridge after ridge, higher and higher and the flat white roofs snuggled amongst the green olive trees. Swannie could hear the unfamiliar sound of running water from a stream high up on the hills. She drank of the fresh, cool water from the spring and how refreshing it was after the flat, earthy tainted and warm water in Boujad. The lovely days were the 'green pastures' for Swannie—streams in the desert and shade over the hot plain. Swannie loved the walled city of Demnate and the people in it from the very first. The mission station itself was outside the city walls and consisted of two narrow buildings each with two or three bedrooms. There was an olive press in the garden and pomegranates supported by Y-shaped sticks. The flowers around were of wonderful colours and at the sight of the mountain range beyond her spirits soared.

As well as working amongst the Berbers living in their homes nearby, she was now able to make regular trips up the Middle Atlas to visit the tiny compounds of black tents dotted all over the hills where the mountain Berbers lived. Some of them moved from the mountains and lived in clay, pink-coloured homes outside the walls of Demnate. The people were poor and many survived by taking on whatever work they could find in the city. The men who were fortunate to have a trade such as shoe-making often bought a small plot of land and grew some olive trees or kept a couple of goats. The women, pretty and vivacious in their youth, married at a young age and started to bear children straightaway, many of whom died in infancy because of poverty and disease. When one child did not survive another was on the way because it was believed that many children were a blessing. But before long the poor mothers were weary and old beyond their years.

As she mixed with the people Swannie became more proficient in their Shilha dialect. Sometimes she borrowed a bicycle, other times she walked the weary miles from Demnate to visit the Berbers in the hills. Often she talked with them well into the night and slept alongside the womenfolk in their portion of the black, goats-hair tents. If it was fine she stayed outside under the stars with a multitude of little 'beasts' for company and a warm blanket to keep out the chilly night air. And as they ate together, using fingers to roll together the couscous or dip bread into a fragrant stew, Swannie noticed the impeccable manners of the Berber mountain people. Rich or poor, old or young, they had the same warm respect for guests who were given the best of everything they had. As the host said the words 'Eat meat' the meal would begin and Swannie soon came to realise that this meat often came from the recently slain, oldest and toughest billy goat ever to climb the Atlas Mountains! But she always gulped and persevered, sometimes tunnelling the pieces of meat way down into the couscous as it was considered quite acceptable to leave a small last portion for those who were serving.

As the years passed Swannie was learning the rules and at the same time gaining the confidence of the Berber people. One day she decided that she would have her own little tent—a bright orange and green one that would stand out bravely from the other big black ones. She could then talk well into the night with the men as well as the women and no one, she hoped, could then complain. According to Swannie's diary those times were some of the best in her life but the time was passing quickly and in 1948 her first furlough was due.

Swannie had a vague feeling that all was not too well at her Missionary Society back in England. She was the first to admit that her own personal vision had changed a lot since leaving for Morocco in 1944. Now she travelled alone into mountainous regions and spent a lot of time living in her tent and speaking to the Berber men as well as teaching the girls and boys in the growing classes at the mission station in Demnate. She was not too sure that the society agreed with her new lifestyle. She had heard that they were fearful for her safety and rather she stayed in the main towns with the other Christians. There would be 'discussions' but Swannie felt sure that their differences could be worked out with the help of prayer.

As Swannie was a skilled artist the B.C.M.S. had asked her to do some drawings of Moroccan scenes, together with a story about Berber life. The whole thing was to be made into an interesting children's painting book and Swannie had worked hard on it and taken much pleasure in the finished product. She was rather looking forward to the admiration and approval of the committee when they saw the sample book.

When she returned home in 1948 her picture book was received with much adulation. But the committee was adamant about one thing; if Swannie were to return to Morocco under the auspices of the British Church Missionary Society, she must adhere to the conditions they specified in full. And one of the conditions was that she did not travel into the Atlas Mountains without a colleague. Swannie was amazed. There were no British missionaries working among the Berbers at that time and she was not only ready and willing to go, but felt convinced that her life's work was amongst them.

She tried to reassure the committee, saying that he had a comfortable little tent of her own now and never travelled without a native boy to guide and help her. Also that she was never too far from the mission station in Demnate. Swannie did go on to tell the committee that she did in fact feel safer with the Berbers in the Middle Atlas than she did walking the streets of London, which may not have gone down too well with the middle-class Englishmen who were unable to compromise. It was becoming more obvious than ever to them that Swannie's vision had changed and her primary commitment now was to the Berbers, particularly those living in the Atlas Mountains. Though they respected her commitment, they did not feel able to condone her trips to those areas, feeling she might be in danger. Swannie understood and appreciated their concern but could only stand by the calling that she knew was from God.

So Swannie's time with the Church Missionary Society came to an unexpected end; there was no alternative for her but to stay in England and once again wait. She found that a very difficult time and her patience was sorely tested. It was two long and painful years before the way opened up for her to return to Morocco and settle down once more to living and working among the people she had grown to love.

But in the early months of 1950 Swannie was invited to join the missionaries based in Meknes under the auspices of the Gospel Missionary Outreach, an American society that had been active in Morocco since 1894. She accepted the invitation on a three-month trial basis and moved to Derb Skat, the mission station in Meknes that had once been a royal palace and was the scene of much G.M.U. activity.

Chapter 5
Settling in Meknes

SO THIS WAS 3, DERB SKAT! Swannie had heard a lot
about the mission station in Meknes from other missionaries;
in fact, she had taken a peep at it herself some years before.
Situated as it was at the end of a narrow dead-end alley, or
derb, with similar dark buildings on either side, it was in the
heart of the old, ancient, still walled city of Meknes. She had
always found it hard to believe that it had once been the palace
of a princess. Now, after stepping through a thick wooden
entrance door that opened as if by magic and then stooping
through a further door, small and arch-shaped, she looked at it
in awe. About 300 years old, it was said to be! Swannie's eyes
were drawn to the spacious tiled courtyard and then upward to
a flat roof some fifty feet or so above with a skylight opening
over the court and an iron grill to keep thieves out. In between
and surrounding the court there was a five-foot balcony
supported by four great columns. Strong railings enclosed the
balcony and straight ahead a small figure leaned over and
waved an excited welcome. It was Ila Davis, a lady missionary

who Swannie had already met and who had been in Morocco with G.M.U. for some years. Swannie's eyes unexpectedly filled with tears at the homely welcome; only she knew how unbearable the two years of waiting had been. She was thrilled to be back in Morocco—and with Derb Skat as her new home.

Swannie turned to the two missionaries who had travelled with her from Middelt where she had lived for a while and could not restrain herself from giving them both a big hug. Bob Schneider and his wife Doris, both young American missionaries, must have chuckled to themselves. They had not thought this was the usual behaviour of a well-brought up young English woman! But they showed their appreciation by hugging her warmly in return and Swannie remained close friends with the Schneiders for many years. In her diary she writes:

> *My reception at Meknes was wonderful and the dear folk are so kind—I slept well last night quietly confident that I was at last in the place God wanted me.*

After the three months were over Swannie wrote to G.M.U. headquarters expressing the hope that she could continue working with them, primarily among the Berbers in the villages and outposts of the Middle Atlas Mountains.

Morocco was at that time still a Protectorate, with fine roads and well-planned towns built by the French who were also progressing with the irrigation of the country. But there seemed to be little spiritual progress though each day commenced as usual with the daily call to prayer in the name of Mohammed.

As the time of Ramadan approached in 1950 Swannie went up one morning onto the roof of the mission station and watched the sun rising. The women in brightly coloured clothes were already working on the rooftops and later would be heard the beating of tom-toms and the firing of canons. The lights would go on up the mosque tower and there would be the sudden blast of trumpets and the chanting of the men inside the mosque. Her heart ached for she knew that most of the usual Berbers who attended would not be present at the meeting in Derb Skat that evening. The pull of Ramadan was too great.

As she settled down in Meknes, Swannie's thoughts centred more and more on how to perfect the Shilha language she had started to learn when staying at the mission station in Demnate. She was determined to start translating some parts of the Bible as soon as she could but needed more help with the Shilha. It came in the form of a little boy who was the son of a shepherd who tended his sheep on the hills outside Meknes. The shepherd became very fond of Swannie, appreciating the way she bravely made her periodic trips up into the hills on her own. He suggested that perhaps his young son could help her with his own dialect while she could teach him some stories out of the Bible. Swannie agreed without any hesitation; this was an opening for which she had waited. She wrote:

> ...*may little Hamid become another reader and a follower of Jesus Christ. How wonderful if I, who have no children, am given Berber sons to train.*

One of the first Berbers Swannie had met on arrival at Meknes was a man who called himself Bousa. He had a full white beard and a wonderfully bright smile and had been led to the Lord as a young man by early G.M.U. missionaries. Bousa was a firm believer and one of ten men put in jail in the early days for refusing to keep the month-long feast of Ramadan. Although many of the menfolk were too afraid to continue attending the mission, Bousa still came and brought his family. They did not live in Meknes but were from the Mijjot tribe and had to travel into the city, which was an hour's walk away.

Swannie immediately loved Bousa's family and their tribe. In those early days she did not drive but took to walking out to Mijjot. Whilst living in Meknes she was missing the freedom

47

of her earlier days and the frequent visits she had been able to make to the hillside Berbers, as an extract from her diary shows:

Much work, study and visiting keep my heart content but a desperate pain shoots through at odd moments for a return to the old, dusty ways of Demnate and the mountain air and happy chatter as I was led through the great mountain splendour.

An opportunity did arise to witness in Meknes at this time, though, in a way that Swannie much appreciated. Mr. Feldman from another Christian organisation decided to put up a Bible booth and distribute literature and Bob Schneider and Swannie were asked to help. With the assistance of Swannie's accordion and Mr. Feldman's musical saw the people crowded round, and then one of the two men would give a short talk. Swannie took this chance to speak in French to some of the schoolgirls who stood on the outskirts of the crowd. They seemed to understand and enjoy the talks but one day she found herself not with the girls as usual but with a group of eight little boys and many young men standing behind them.

A French general passed and Swannie held her breath. Would he be displeased with her for what might be termed 'proselyting' and was not legal under the French regime? He paused and stopped to listen and then, to Swannie's delight he came across and shook her hand. Then he enquired whether any Bibles had been sold and a conversation ensued into which the two men joined. They were very late home that night and had much to tell their colleagues!

In August of that first year with G.M.U. Swannie found herself in a much quieter Derb Skat than usual as Bob and Doris Schneider and their twins were visiting Tangier for a few weeks.

She and Ila Davies were alone but not for long. To Swannie's delight quite a few of their colleagues working in other places came to stay with them unexpectedly. She had the chance to meet Pete Friessen and his wife again and also Maud Cary, an older missionary of many years' standing, who stayed with them for a week and of whom Swannie was particularly fond. Miss Cary was a single lady who, like herself, was fond of all kinds of literature and wrote very acceptable poetry. She became a real friend to Swannie, who poured out her fears and aspirations in a way that she had never been able to do before and was given kind and loving advice from the more mature missionary.

When Swannie had been in Demnate in earlier years, she had established a class for young boys who were still very much on her heart. The boys were now older but she had continued to keep in touch with some of them, especially those who were eager to perfect their English. One or two stayed close to Swannie over the years and later became co-workers in the important work of translation and radio broadcasting that she was able to do.

In March 1950 it was Swannie's fortieth birthday. She had heard nothing from her family at home and had to admit to feeling rather sad and homesick. She was spending a few days at the mission station in Sefrou at the time and was amazed when her colleagues surprised her with a party and a large birthday cake. Swannie almost wept—she would willingly try to survive under the most difficult circumstances but how she loved a party and how it eased her loneliness. When she returned to Meknes there were yet more cards and the present of a lovely red shopping bag. 'What dear, dear folk my American colleagues are…' she wrote in her diary for that day.

Later that year Swannie had the opportunity of going up again into the hills to Mijjot with Bob Schneider and his wife. Bob's car had to be parked some distance from the black Berber tents because of the dangerous mountain paths and the walk brought back to Swannie poignant memories of the time she had spent in Demnate years before. A song seemed to be let loose in her heart as she remembered again the feeling of freedom that took over as she rode slowly on the back of a mule with her little tent packed away and one of the young boys close beside her to lead the way. The first five years Swannie had spent in Morocco were vibrant and exciting and would always be very precious in her memories.

During this visit Swannie had the privilege of meeting Ben Ashir, a Berber friend whom she had met before when first living in Meknes. At that time she and Bob had been character witnesses in the trial of Ben Ashir's father who was accused of some petty crime. He had been released and both father and son were extremely grateful.

And what a lovely character Swannie was finding Ben Ashir to be. He was extremely kind and gentle with his wife and family and moved about with a quiet dignity that really impressed Swannie. In the evenings they would sit outside his tent, talking and reading together and then sharing some native dish with his wife and family. Swannie loved this healthy outdoor life and the many opportunities it provided to talk freely about her own faith. They were such busy days, moving from tent to tent giving medicine, teaching to read and generally helping where she could and each night she would lie thankfully down under a blanket and sleep soundly, despite the hard bed of earth and the cloud of persistent insects.

One day Ben Ashir asked if he could take Swannie up the hills to see a particularly beautiful mountain spring. As they trotted home contentedly at sunset, Swannie sitting on the mule and Ben Ashir walking alongside, he spoke of his longing now to be a witness to the gospel among his own people. Swannie wrote in her diary that night of 'Grace Astounding!' and could hardly bear to leave the mountain village.

But a surprise was in store for Swannie. Si Mohammed was worried for her safety and also for her health in the winter months. He promised to have a small nuella (thatched hut) built for her so that she could come back into the hills whenever she pleased. It would be near his family's own big black tent so that there would always be someone near and Swannie thanked him with tears in her eyes. She could hardly believe that at last she was going to have a little home of her own—and in the midst of her beloved Berber friends.

By late November Swannie's dear little nuella was almost finished and she could hardly wait to stamp her own personality on it. Other young men were helping with the building of the nuella by this time and she longed to be able to stay and teach them all to read. She hoped that none of her American colleagues would raise objections to her living for weeks at a time in the hills, as the English Missionary Society had done, but Swannie thought not. Anyhow, she had been reading books on the lives of such women as Mary Slessor and Lilias Trotter who were used greatly in very unconventional conditions.

They had moved ahead in their work despite the criticism of others because they knew that the only permission needed was from God. Swannie took assurance from that fact and when the last day of 1950 arrived wrote in her diary:

I can testify before this book closes that God has been faithful in his promises to me. He has led me and kept me. I am warm, fed, and nearer my precious Berbers than ever before. My nuella is a fact, my language progresses and though I may have aroused adverse criticism, I cannot live in concord with all if it means separating myself from the trust of the people I have come to Morocco to serve. It is 10.45 p.m. and we are nearly in another year. I will read for a while.

Chapter 6
A Glimpse at the Berbers

THE ATLAS MOUNTAINS LIE IN NORTHWESTERN Africa and are an extension of the European Alps. The highest range in the chain is to be found in southern Morocco and is called the High or Grand Atlas; the second highest peak is to be found in the Middle Atlas. Both the High and Middle Atlas slopes have dense forests containing cedar, pine, cork and oak trees but there are fertile valley and pastureland where livestock can feed. Traditionally, the Atlas Mountains are considered Berber territory.

There are many different Berber tribes and in the Middle Atlas the mother tongue is mainly Shilha. They were originally a nomadic people and lived on the hillside in large black tents woven from goats' hair and wool, together with the fibre of the palmetto plants gathered by the women, spun and then weaved into strips. These are boiled in pomegranate peelings to preserve the tents from the bad weather and because the peelings hold a natural dye the Berber tents are always black. The men traditionally sew the strips together and raise the tent, rolling up the sides in hot weather to allow the breeze to pass through and closing them in the winter cold. The whole family—boys, girls, mothers, fathers, babies, grandparents—all live together in the one tent divided into sections.

The kitchen and workroom is the women's domain and usually contains an iron tripod to place over the campfire, fuel, cooking utensils and a flat basket for bread. Not many eating utensils would be there, just a couple of soup bowls, the occasional spoon and a flat tray for serving the meal. But every home would have a shiny copper kettle, a teapot and some small glasses, mint tea being an essential even in the poorest homes.

The women's sleeping quarters would be quite separate from those of the men, the latter using theirs not only for sleeping in but for sitting round and talking over the issues of the day. The women's gathering place was usually the nearest well as they did all their laundry there and also filled huge goatskins with water to take back for the family's domestic use.

It was in Mijjot, a small Berber settlement in the Middle Atlas, that Swannie first started visiting the people in their large black tents. They became very fond of her as she chatted to the women as they tackled their household tasks and to the men as they sat outside their tents in the evenings. Gradually she learned more of their language and at first Swannie slept in the women's section of one of the huge tents but then decided to buy herself a small, coloured tent which she pitched next to the black ones. But the nights were often bitterly cold and the Berber men realised that as she was not used to tent life she should have a warmer place to spend the nights. When the little, one-roomed hut with a thatched roof was built for her it allowed Swannie to spend many happy months among them from early 1951 until late 1954 when it had to be abandoned because of internal strife and subsequent danger to foreigners.

Many of the cities were ancient Berber marketing centres for the hill people and the Berber men were often able to speak

Arabic as well as Shilha, though very few women left their hillside homes. Meknes was such a city, together with Khemisset, Sefrou and El Hajeb. As the years passed many families decided to leave their hard nomadic life and set up their homes in the towns, so there was an ever-increasing Berber population.

When Swannie arrived in Meknes in 1950 the G.M.U. had mission stations in each of the above towns. As early as 1905 missionaries had used the mountain town of Sefrou, an inland town south of Fes, as a base to contact Berbers. During the French occupation it became a 'new city' for French officials and had a large Jewish population as well as Arab and Berber. During World War II the mission had closed because of lack of personnel but after the war a couple of missionaries returned from furlough and it opened again. G.M.U. also owned land just outside Sefrou but had been denied a building permit. When the religious climate changed and they were at last given permission to build it was decided that a language study centre was necessary. Eventually it was built and over the years Sefrou became an exciting outreach centre with many students.

El Hajeb is a small Berber town built on the cliffs below the evergreen forests and under French rule became a summer resort, with winter ski facilities. As the town is approached by road a great mass of rock in the shape of an eyebrow looms up in front, and that is how the town first got its name—el hajeb, the eyebrow. There was great resistance to G.M.U. renting a house there at first but finally a small one was made available. At the grand age of seventy Miss Maud Carey, one of the first missionaries to respond to the call of Morocco in the early years of the 20th century, moved from Derb Skat in Meknes to take on the new challenge. Later the mission was able to buy a house in El Hajeb instead of renting.

Khemmiset was just a small town when G.M.U. bought the first property but the French had built a hospital, post office, bus station, police station, a French school and some government buildings. Most of the homes were nuellas which were originally round mud huts with grass thatched roofs or more progressively oblong rooms and corrugated tin roofs. European immigration was being encouraged and Khemisset was quickly developing. Because of this a villa was able to be purchased by G.M.U. in the French quarter with the advantage of a big walled-in yard. It became a very busy mission station with classes being held for girls living in the neighbourhood and also those who were residing in the home of Ellen Doran and Emmagen Coats, two single American missionaries. These two ladies taught the girls English from the Bible as well as more practical subjects. Later they looked after the children at the Ain Leuh Orphanage for many years.

Swannie was able to help at each of these mission stations at certain times. One of the missionaries might be going home on furlough or another of the young married women could be expecting a baby and needing help. Whatever it was, Swannie was only too eager to help and in so doing gain knowledge of different areas and customs. It also helped her become more acquainted with her colleagues as she moved from place to place. She enjoyed travelling around but was glad to have a base at Derb Skat where she had her own little room and privacy. She was seldom lonely as many people passed through and Swannie also took every opportunity she could to go out to the uneducated Berber people in the Middle Atlas villages.

She often biked out to Mijjot, as mentioned earlier, and in that first year at Derb Skat had the privilege of spending a whole month in the Middle Atlas with Ila Davies, a colleague also living at Derb Skat. Swannie was intent at this time in perfecting the Shilha language and was especially eager to start a school to teach the children. They had been invited by Berber friends living in Mjjot to spend some time with them so set off, complete with tent, cans of food, towels, primus stoves and a radio. When they arrived the Berber men immediately helped them put up their little tent.

Meanwhile Swannie and Ila had a problem—toilet facilities! The Berber women simply went out into the fields but the two missionaries were either too modest or just too western for that. So they hung a curtain in the corner of the tent and put a bucket behind it. At night while everyone slept, they emptied the bucket!

Soon they were able to hold a small clinic every morning and mothers came from many miles away to get salve for their children's eyes or some medicine for themselves or their menfolk. Swannie was beginning to understand a little of what they were saying and, much to her astonishment, they were beginning to understand her.

In fact, one day Swannie was so good that as she told some of the men about England where she had been born, she finished by commenting: 'It is an island—a place surrounded by water!'

Many pairs of eyes gazed up at her in wonder. Then one old man said incredulously, 'But where do you grow your crops and how do you manage to live?'

Swannie loved to talk to the children and often drew pictures to help them understand what she meant. These were often shown to the women as she talked while they made bread outside the tents and then baked it on the round clay ovens standing about four feet high. When they had finished they would make Swannie a hot, sweet glass of mint tea and as they drank together the women would excitedly chatter. It was a hard life for the Berber women who were given in marriage at a very early age for the dowry payment and became mothers when they were sometimes as young as twelve or thirteen years of age. The girls had little childhood and were soon victims of drudgery and primitive household tasks that were handed over to them when they married. It was an unexpected treat for them to sit and talk to the foreign ladies.

Swannie always thought the Berbers were fortunate to live outside in the open, enjoying the warmth of the sunshine and the green grass and flowers. But the Berber women envied the city people, especially on cold winter nights when wind and muddy rain had to be endured. During Ramadan life was always extremely dangerous but in 1951 Swannie noticed that many Berber Christians were making the night journey from Mijjot to Derb Skat to avoid the ritual feasts that took place after a day of fasting. Evelyn Stenbock, herself a missionary with G.M.U. for several years, was at the time staying at Derb Skat and recalls: 'It was late at night, well after dark, during Ramadan. One by one Berber men from the Mijjot tribe rapped on the door and slipped into the house until the room was filled with these dear countrymen who risked their lives to hear the Word of God. It was a thrilling sight for us all.'

But the dark winter passed and in the early spring, when the ground was covered with flowers and the hills were becoming green and lush once again, Swannie was taken to her nuella—the first home that was exclusively her own. There are pictures of this home and Swannie's diary records that she wept as she went into the little room, bare except for mattress, cushions and a little stove that the women had supplied.

Soon Swannie made the nuella very cosy and completely her own by first painting a text to go behind the little bed on the rough stone wall. Then she placed her little brass kettle and teapot on the long low table she had been given, ready to make mint tea for the many visitors she was expecting. And when she was given a rug of goats' wool for the floor Swannie laughed and said how warm she would be—Somebody up there must certainly know how her knees ached on the hard floor when she was praying!

Swannie's devotion to the Berbers was all-consuming and evident to all. One of her fellow missionaries, John Barcus, wrote in a letter to England:

...it did seem to me that Swannie felt everyone else should have the same priority in his or her missionary endeavour! But Swannie would ride on bicycle, motorbike, bus, jeep or mule to get out of the city and reach the country folk. She lived and slept with them, ate their food, spoke their tongue and desired earnestly to translate the Scriptures into their dialect. Some of the stories she related about life among HER *people astounded me.*

One of these stories was related to me by another missionary couple and shows the depth of Swannie's compassion for the Berber people and her desire to show them the love of Christ by serving them. Twins had been born to one of the women and, as she had only enough milk to feed one baby and the custom was to keep the stronger of the two, she felt she must abandon the other. When Swannie heard what was happening she immediately placed the abandoned baby in her nuella and rode the several miles into Meknes on her bicycle to buy canned milk and other supplies needed to keep the little boy alive. One morning she decided to bathe him. To the consternation of the women of the village whose custom it was not to bathe their own babies until they were much older, sometimes twelve months old. They congregated outside Swannie's nuella in amazement, waiting with wide-open eyes and bated breath to see what would happen to the little baby. However, he lived for many years to tell the tale and the incident made a lasting impression on the womenfolk. They were learning to trust Swannie more and more.

Everyone was welcome in Swannie's nuella and her mint tea was gaining a reputation. When Don and Irma Peterson arrived as new missionaries in July 1951, a couple of colleagues took them from Casablanca to Meknes and later out to Mijjot where Swannie was living. She immediately invited them into her nuella and served them their first good Moroccan mint tea along with some delicious cookies.

They loved it! The couple went to work at the mission

station in Sefrou but eleven months later Irma was in Meknes for the birth of their first baby. Swannie went into the delivery room to stay beside her as it was a difficult breech birth and prayed without ceasing! Perhaps a more spiritual than practical helper on this occasion but the young parents never forgot her loving care. When the missionaries began to be expelled from Morocco, Don and Irma Peterson were assigned to Alaska. What a joy it was for them to have Swannie stay at their home when she visited the USA for deputation work in 1969. Irma recalls that '...our first visit with Swannie was in *her* home in Morocco and our last visit with her was in *our* home in Alaska.'

So from 1951 Swannie was able to stay among the Mijjot tribe and sleep comfortably in her own little bed. During this time she opened up a school for boys and as she taught them to read, her own language skills improved. Her mind was never far from the problem of lack of literature of any kind in the Berber tongue as at that time the language was not officially recognised in Morocco. It was then that she started to think around the possibility of translating a portion of the Bible, possibly the Gospel of Luke or John or the Psalms, into the Shilha dialect. She was beginning to notice also that transistor radios were becoming very popular with the people. If a man was able to obtain one from the city, he would take it back to the village and the whole encampment would gather and listen enthralled. Swannie's active mind began to take in another possibility. Radio outreach to the Berber tribes could reach up into many hill country sites and the Gospel message could be heard even by the women, who in most cases could not read.

Swannie's vision was bright and clear—she must consistently keep on with the practical work she was able to do and ask guidance for further outreach which seemed to point to radio work as well as translation of Scriptures into the Shilha language.

Chapter 7
Independence Again

THE MOROCCAN KING WHO HAD BEEN responsible for the 1912 treaty with France had his own personal reasons for doing so. He had called in European help to subdue his own warring tribes and keep his own dynasty on the throne. The French had agreed not to propagate Christianity but there were no restrictions placed on European worship. The agreement allowed no proselytising among Muslims.

The French took little notice of this clause and under French rule evangelical missionaries managed to witness and still be in favour with the government. France had obtained a vast new region of fertile land and during the protectorate years the Berbers, who were the original inhabitants and whom the Arabs had failed to subdue, proved to be competent and cheap farm labourers. With the help of European farming methods the arid Sahara south of the Atlas Mountains became a valley of roses cultivated for French perfume while central Morocco was ideal for jasmine and other rare fragrances. There were the natural cork forests and an endless supply of wine produced from the vineyards that the French planted. Melons, plums, cherries, apricots, citrus fruits and vegetables filled the fields and orchards.

France was changing Morocco into a modern civilisation. They built roads, railways, hospitals, schools, libraries and orphanages. When the Arabs had taken over North Africa in the seventh century the Berbers remained hostile, always a law onto themselves and almost impossible to bring under control. France had succeeded in some measure by cultivating their skills and educating their children.

Peace prevailed for several years, but as Berbers moved on into government and supervisory jobs, the Arabs began to protest and conflict began once again. By 1949 an uprising had occurred and Morocco moved into a state of revolution. Europeans became the target of unprovoked attacks as the nationalistic spirit grew. The Sultan of Morocco tried to get rid of all foreign influences but in 1953, with a view to stopping terrorism, the French banished him from the country.

The people went into deep mourning and the terrorism increased. Swannie and many other missionaries plodded on with their day-by-day tasks but there was growing uneasiness. None of the mission stations had been touched and there was no thought at that time of leaving the country. But as the summer wore on there were many violent demonstrations in small towns like El Hajeb and Khemisset. Many people were fleeing from the country in terror and Meknes was the scene of murders and rioting when the new French ruler visited. Association with foreigners might bring death so attendance at the mission stations dropped dramatically.

The beautiful Moroccan fields were blackened where the grain ripening for harvest had been burnt down, farms and houses were nothing but burned-out shells as the nationalists demanded the return of their sultan and independence for their country.

Then on 2nd March, 1956, after much bloodshed and

tragedy, the French gave the country back to its Arab rulers and the exiled Sidi Muhammad Ben Youssef, Sultan of Morocco, was brought back from his enforced exile in Corsica and Madagascar. The pent-up excitement of a whole nation exploded into 'Yahiya El Malik!'(Long Live the King) as the Moroccans rejoiced.

Would independence hurt the missionary? Many of them thought it would, although the king himself was tolerant and exhorted his people to '…remain faithful to the Islam virtues of justice, tolerance, sense of duty, respect for the human person.' But a new flood of religious fervour was sweeping the country. Swannie found herself involved in this when she was travelling back home by train with a friend, Verna. They had received an unexpected invitation to stay in Tangier for a few days and the station in Meknes had been left empty. While on their return journey a riot broke out in Meknes. They knew nothing of this until they enquired why the train was going straight through to Fes and not stopping at Meknes as planned. Immediately she knew Swannie contacted her co-workers in Khemisset knowing they would be fearful for the safety of the two women who they thought were still at Derb Skat. In Meknes store windows were broken and the streets smeared with blood as rioters used broken glass to slash the throats of helpless victims. God had protected the missionaries in a wonderful way and not one of them was hurt. Order was finally restored in Meknes but the missionaries could feel the bitter hatred that was developing towards those from the western world. A few months later Swannie was in Khemisset having a meal with some of her colleagues in the home of an English-trained nurse when a bomb exploded outside. They rushed to help at the nearby hospital and found Arab friends of theirs as well as Berber boys from the school classes badly injured. Many of them did not survive.

At the end of 1956 Morocco was made a member of the United Nations and it seemed the frightening years of rioting and massacre were coming to an end. The G.M.U. missionaries were able to meet for a prayer conference in September 1956 and praised God for his protection though acknowledging that the way was still very unclear. Many felt that God was preparing them for a greater work in Morocco than ever before and Swannie herself was filled with excitement at a new challenge. She had become more convinced than ever that the written word was vital if any real progress was to be made with the Berbers.

Because of the difficult situation Swannie was forced to leave her precious little nuella on the hillside when the king returned from exile. For four years she had lived there among the Berber people and a school had been started. Countless opportunities had arisen when Swannie could chat with the women and girls as they carried out heavy household chores and carried pitchers of water from the well. In the evenings she had been able to sit with the men outside the big black tents and talk, always bringing in the truths of the gospel. Swannie treasured those years for they endeared her to the Berbers who gave her much love and affection as well as practical help in her language study. The hours she spent talking with them were a great boon in helping her perfect the pronunciation of the difficult Shilha dialect, invaluable in her later radio broadcasts.

Because of Swannie's caring spirit as well as her words, many of the Berbers from Mijjot came to believe in the Christian message. They trusted Swannie but it was not easy to make a decision to serve Christ in a Muslim country such as Morocco and though there were many professions of faith it was only a change in lifestyle that made an impression on Swannie. For example, she knew more than most how easy it was for a Berber to tell lies. In fact they were so astonished at her truthfulness that they laughingly called her a name in Berber that translated into English roughly means 'One whose yes is yes and whose no is no!' She was not easily taken in by promises or words and as she taught the children to read and write Swannie also warned them of the dangers of lying.

When she was compelled to leave her nuella Swannie still continued her morning classes in Meknes and some of the Berber boys travelled out from Mijjot to continue their lessons. There were classes for the girls, too, but they usually lived locally in Meknes. Often there would be as many as fifteen giggling, curious girls listening wide-eyed to the Bible stories and trying hard to learn the words of songs so that they could join in. They liked to sing but Swannie's desire was to teach them to read because so quickly they would be married and no longer little girls willing to be taught but women dependent upon the whims of their husbands. This was not an easy task because girls were expected to help with all the household chores as well as look after their younger brothers and sisters, leaving them with far less free time than the boys. A verse memorised from the Bible or copied out in Shilha was a great achievement for the girl herself and also for Swannie.

At marriageable age the real problems started. One of the girls lived in a house almost alongside Derb Skat and came from a large Moroccan family. The children all attended classes when they were small but as this particular girl grew older, she decided she had learnt enough! It was only later when she saw her friends still meeting together at Derb Skat that she remembered the kindness of the missionary ladies and how happy she had been with them. She asked Swannie if she could meet with the group once again and permission was granted. This time she listened to the lessons with real interest. She was a clever girl who had been educated as a Muslim and was now eager to test out for herself the things she was hearing. Swannie gave her a Bible and she literally fell in love with it. She couldn't put it down and as she read she made a decision to follow the Christian way.

She told her parents but suffered no persecution in the home because the missionaries had helped her mother out often in difficult circumstances. But very soon came the inevitable question—who would she marry? She was then only thirteen and did not want to give up her freedom to marry a stranger and be ruled by a mother-in-law she had not yet met. She understood well enough that once she was married she would have to go to her new husband's home and would almost certainly be treated like a slave there. The situation was even more devastating for a girl who had taken up the Christian faith. Her marriage would put a stop to any classes she wanted to attend and her new Muslim family would persecute her for what she believed. The girl was in tears when she told the missionaries that the parents of a prospective groom were coming to visit her home. They would bring many gifts and proceed to barter for the girl's hand during an evening carefully planned by her parents. The girl herself would take no part in the proceedings though many questions would be asked about her. As the men sat in a separate room the women of the household would take note of the smallest details of the potential mother-in-law. Was she haughty, or sarcastic? Was her manner genuinely kind or would she be different once the honeymoon ended? Did her son have other wives? Did he drink? Did he pray?

But all these considerations would come to nothing if the men agreed on a price. The real action was in the men's room and once they struck a deal it would be nearly impossible to change, despite the girl's feelings or that of her mother. There were three evenings of barter before the girl's fate would be decided.

There had been a new law introduced in Morocco just before that time, legally allowing a girl to accept or reject a marriage proposal. After the bargaining had been completed she apparently had the freedom to say no. But so strong were the old customs that rarely did a girl object to her father's decision. When this particular girl was asked what she thought, she just stared at the floor and didn't say a word. Her silence was taken for approval and the engagement contract was signed. Tearfully, she poured out her story to the missionaries in Derb Skat but it was too late. She had now become the property of the man she was to marry and could not travel or visit without his consent, even though up to that time she had not met him.

Swannie attended many wedding feasts while she was in Morocco. Some of these were between young people who had accepted the Christian faith and gave her great joy. Weddings in Morocco were always huge, ceremonious events and even in poor Berber villages they would go on for several days and the bride would wear many different dresses. She often made the dresses herself as Moroccan girls were taught at an early age how to sew and embroider and often did it with great skill. The wedding would begin on Friday, the Muslim holy day, and continue for the whole weekend. Catering was an immense job and the cooking took place on Saturday with the butchering of the cow or sheep, or perhaps a hundred chickens, done the day before. An immense amount of fresh bread was made by the women and dozens of cases of soft drinks purchased.

Throughout the weekend while the guests made merry the bride sat in a room by herself dressed in her gorgeous clothes. Every time she changed into a different dress she had to parade in the courtyard to let the guests admire her, and then they themselves went away to change in the hope of having their pictures taken with the bride.

Swannie and other missionaries attending such weddings usually arrived at the close of the festivities and accompanied the bride to the groom's house or waited with the groom until she arrived. On Sunday morning the bride would change into her last outfit and, traditionally, be carried through the streets to meet the bridegroom for the first time.

If the couple were Berber Christians the families of the young people often insisted on Berber customs being kept but later, after the meal and festivities, a Christian marriage service would be conducted.

So life went on as usual for many of the missionaries despite the revolution and constant threat of expulsion. It was to be some time before Swannie was told explicitly to leave the country although in the intervening years many of her colleagues were ordered to go.

Chapter 8
A Trip Up the High Atlas

IN THE MID-1950S SWANNIE WAS ABLE to plan an extended trip out among the Berbers in the High Atlas Mountains. With her went her friend Kaye, a midwife from England, and two other missionaries from Meknes accompanied them for part of the way. One of them, Al Jessup, had not worked specifically among the Berbers before and his comments when asked were that he was there for a short time mainly 'to observe and learn.' The purpose of the visit was to share the love of Christ by means of message and medicine and as such Kaye and Swannie were a very special team.

As usual Swannie kept a diary of this visit, illustrated again with her own drawings and written in her own inimitable style of illustrative writing. The diary gives an insight into the character of Swannie that no other person could do. I think you will agree that this special account should be left in diary form again, with only an apology that the very amusing illustrations done by Swannie cannot be reproduced because they have become faded somewhat by time. But as usual she describes the incidents and places so colourfully that they immediately fire our imagination.

So we depart with Swannie and her colleagues in her Landrover to spend a month in the High Atlas Mountains:

Monday, 21 May
We arrived in Demnate at 5.30 p.m. after a good journey from Meknes, stopping at Boujad for lunch where we were very warmly welcomed. Boujad has its attractions but not now for me. The town seems to have lost some of the character I found there in my first years in Morocco. It was good to see Si Mohammed again. Their garden is beautiful with roses, lupins, sweet peas, geraniums and the tall hollyhocks I have always found so beautiful here.

Wednesday, 23 May
I am on the open road again—a narrow mountain road. If only for a few days I eat what I can, where I can and how I can! Sleep is where we stop for the night and a bed is no necessity. We did wonder at the last minute whether we could go because a French ordinance survey party had been refused permission to go into the mountains because of the general insecurity of the whole area. But we saw the captain of the Nationalist Party and managed to procure from him two letters to certain notable Berbers promising hospitality. So we started off and I knew with certainty that no man was going to shut this open door.

Saturday, 26 May
We took the jeep as far as it would go—about thirty kilometres. When the road was no longer passable we hired mules. Then sat on top of our baggage and travelled with the men who were to be our guides. We journeyed for some hours to the village of Tizin Oubadou. We found the sheik of Oubadou very offhand though we ate butter and honey with him and two or three other men. Kaye gave out some medicines while we talked with the men and read to them.

69

Sunday, 27 May
We were awakened at six o'clock this morning by one of the guides—a handsome rascal by the name of Brahim. We call him Brahim II since his companion has the same name as he is older and has to be Brahim I! Kaye treated some callers while I had further opportunity to talk to one of the men who had listened last night and showed considerable interest. Last night a little lad about six years old was brought on a mule by his uncle having just had all his clothes accidentally set on fire. He was horribly burnt with no skin left on his poor little body from his knees to his throat. After treatment by Kaye, I carried him out to his uncle who lifted him onto the mule. For a minute it all seemed so strange, standing in the moonlight by those mountain homes and lifting up a little Berber lad to the dark Berber face looking down at me, and then fumbling my way back down dark stairs and completely black passage to the candle-lit room where we were staying. Strange, and yet so utterly satisfying. We stopped for lunch with the sheik of Timlookin-Hammou and then rode on to Tisent, passing by an empty Jewish village. We sent the mules back at Tisent and drank tea with a handsome elderly Berber called El Aid. He offered us a room in exchange for medicine. We went on to Asbashkoo and met Sheik Idal and his wife Mahajuba. We were given an extra large key for our room that was so unusual I had to draw it!

Monday, 28 May
Last night we sat with Sheik Idal and his wife and ate harira (a kind of porridge) and couscous. This glum old Sheik took his wife from the bad house in Demnate because he thought she was pregnant. She is an Arab—looks like a painted doll and has little crafty eyes that dart about furtively. She is no longer young but obviously makes a grim effort to hold back the receding years. It was a shock to the sheik when he found out that there was no baby after all! He had actually bought all the food for the feast to be held for the baby's arrival. Mahajuba (the wife) declares sorcery has been practised upon her and that is the reason she has no

baby! She is disliked by the entire neighbourhood for her imperious behaviour and because she was the cause of the sheik divorcing his first wife who was a respectable Berber woman. Our room is a large old attic with a balcony outside looking down upon the river—icy cold and very swift—thundering over the boulders day and night. There is only candlelight. After breakfast we went to Tisent and visited the nearby homes. We met a woman in a deep blue dress and red headscarf. She had a remarkable face—high cheekbones, a huge mouth, great yellow teeth with many gaps, and one eye out of action with a white ulcer. But the other eye was so vivacious—it twinkled and danced. She was positively fascinating!

Tuesday, 29 May
We had breakfast with the sheik and his wife—a long dull affair of nearly two hours—coffee—har'rra—tea—rice and melted butter—more tea. I spoke to Mahajuba in her room afterwards. She has no sense of need and quite content with all she hopes Mohammed can do for her. We went afterwards to Tisent again and I talked with a woman in Shilha and was gratified to realise I could make myself understood. When El Aid turned up I talked and read with him for some time and when a very fine looking Berber by the name of Hammou came in, he repeated to him all I had said. Hammou had brought with him his very pretty wife for treatment. She wears her hair as all the women do in this area, cut to chin level and hanging each side of the face. The back is left long and plaited under a scarf. We went back and had dinner with Mahajuba as the sheik was away for the day. His son, Si Omar arrived, looking very dashing in his white rezza and silver dagger in its sheath. We heard that the Army of Liberation had intended to spend the night here but changed their mind. I was disappointed—it would have been interesting to see what they would have done with two English women!

Wednesday, 30 May
Last night while Kaye was out doing medicine I sat with the women cooking round the fire. After speaking about Jesus,

71

Mahajuba said with perfect contentment 'Our prophet does all that for us and more. He takes us in to heaven in spite of all our sin—that doesn't matter!'

This morning Mahajuba had a row with the sheik. Several people came for medicine and after dinner when we had rested we went to see a woman who was desperately ill. She had an infected womb after childbirth and had a racing pulse and temperature of 104. Kaye had begun to treat her but it seemed humanly impossible for her to stay alive in the filthy room where she lived. We prayed aloud and in her family's presence for God to spare her and her little baby. Mahajuba had told me about the father. Apparently everyone thought he was demon-possessed but he was very courteous when I talked to him. I met a man who makes strange keys, probably that was where our extraordinarily big one came from!

Thursday, 31 May

This morning we heard that the Army of Liberation had returned and taken four women to prison. Last night I spoke to the father of a little boy who seems to have attached himself to me. He is a Jew now converted to Islam and altogether most unlikeable. He tries hard to be a devout Moslem but can't hide the fact that he is a profound rogue. Our prayer was answered regarding the fakeeh's wife. Her pulse rate came down but then one of the women gave the baby a glass of dettol that had been left for the sick mother to wash in. She thought it was tea! At Tisent today I talked at length to a hadj (a man who has made the pilgrimage to Mecca). I read to him a portion from Revelation and he seemed most interested. After a rest Kaye and I went to the other side of the river as I wanted to photograph the house. We went across a stone onbridge crossing the river beyond Tisent where the valley widens, giving a lovely view of Bou Gnas. We arrived back as it was getting dark but went to see how the baby who swallowed the dettol was. He had recovered! There was a conference here today with the sheik, the men coming from all around. It was something to do with the proximity of the Army of Liberation. Strange that I feel so free at this time and in such a place, with no other European except us for miles across the rugged mountain terrain.

Friday, 1 June

I did a drawing of the son of the hadj who makes the picturesque shoes that women here wear. We went to see his work before leaving Tisent but his father, in order to show his Moslem zeal, rose and went out rather than drink tea with such blasphemers as we two women.

El Aid is a most good-natured fellow but is really rather exasperating as he insists on holding tea parties in the room where he said we could treat patients—filling the room with flies and making it embarrassing for women to consult Kaye regarding treatment. But he is very kind to us, especially considering the fact that the unfriendly Hadj is his brother.

Saturday, 2 June

Breakfast as usual with the sheik and Mahajuba. They both seem peeved and behave as if it is our fault there is no baby. The young son wanted me to take his photograph so I went on the roof with him and he pulled off his rezza, brushed up his revolutionary hair and stripped off his shallaba to reveal European garb underneath. Then he threw his arm round his little wife in most un-Moslem fashion and posed looking a positive rake! The old sheik would have beheaded him had he known but the young man kisses his father's shoulder in deference, winks at his little wife and sits in meek silence. But I fear he will paint the fortress red when the old man dies and it will become as full of noise and laughter then as it is strained and joyless now.

Sunday, 3 June

This morning we walked to the village of Agourama in Assameur and had a very cordial welcome from the Adil's brother, Ahmed. It was a tiring walk because it was chiefly uphill and the sun was strong but the scenery was magnificent which

73

made it easier to forget the aching body! We met the Adil on the way back—a very capable, intelligent Berber. He came along on his mule with an attendant running beside him. It was a much easier journey back downhill and we avoided a precarious bit of path that I had disliked on the way up.

Monday, 4 June

We went to Tisent and stared to bargain for the use of some mules the next day. We had not intended leaving Abashkoo yet but feel the situation is getting too tense to remain. While waiting for Kaye to clear up the medicine, the boys came out of the mosque school and gathered round. I read to them and they were quiet and attentive. I spoke in Arabic and Shilha to be sure they all understood. Suddenly a thick-set man appeared and asked me what I was teaching the lads. I said that I was explaining about sinful behaviour and instead of dispersing the boys he became interested and listened himself!

Tuesday 5th June

El Aid brought the mules about 9 a.m. but Idal and Mahajuba didn't even leave the room to see us off. Had the baby existed we would have left with all honours.

We took a tortuous and sometimes comical path to the Tizi crisscrossing the river several times. A man with a gun joined us soon after we left. All guns had to be handed in two days ago so we thought he was from the Army of Liberation. He was uncommunicative at first but thawed out on the way. Up the Pass of Tizi Tirlist we photographed some very ancient engravings on a slab of rock. The snow was just above us and a great wind blew. We sat together eating bread and butter and hard-boiled eggs and reached the Adil's house in Tirsal about 2 p.m. The Adil was away so his brother Omar entertained us.

Wednesday, 6 June

Last night I slept very badly. The cement floor was so hard after such a long time on the mule yesterday. I lay awake and wondered if I were lying on that part of the matting under which I had seen a woman most generously spit the night before! I wish I could cease to be so fastidious and develop the Berber mind more thoroughly. Last evening the fakeeh Si Ahmed came and asked for the book we promised last Saturday. This morning Omar, who looks rather like a Roman senator, asked me to explain the illustrations in a 'Reader's Digest,' which I did. His lips curled openly in contempt when I mentioned the Bible for he was familiar with the Christian message. But when we were leaving he put one hand on my shoulder, gripped my hand with the other, and said softly, 'Please come back.'

Thursday, 7 June
I had a long talk last evening with the son-in-law of the sheik. He is a soldier but was on a brief leave. He climbed up on to the roof where I was sitting and we talked until the sun went down and the stars came out. We discussed the prevalence of sin and the need of sacrifice. The heights of Asseloun grew gaunt and shadowy in the distance and the goats became quiet on the road beneath. It was another conversation that I shall always remember.

We have a lovely room here and it is good to sleep at last on a mattress. This evening we went for a walk to a lovely glade where there were orchids, wild gladioli, tansy, buttercups, viper's bugloss—a sort of scarlet pimpernel, lady-slippers, wild thyme and sage. I saw a little fly curled up in a daisy. He looked so exceedingly comfortable that he inspired a poem (part of the poem is at the end of this chapter). I spoke with some pretty women who cut their hair in a fringe and wear much old silver jewellery. Returning from the walk, I saw a little shepherd lad bringing home the flock from a high pasturage where they had been since early morning—a terrible journey up through crags and forest area. He counted them and I questioned, 'Suppose one is missing?' He answered, 'Then I must go back there tonight and search...' Would the Good Shepherd do less?

Friday, 8 June
This morning I went by myself back along the path to where I had seen the little mosque school on the way to this sheik's house. I sat on a stone by the stream and prayed for the fakeeh and the children of the neighbourhood. When I returned I went upstairs and sat with the women and talked with them and the wife of the sheik, Lilla Fatima. She is an educated Arab lady so I used her to interpret. She is a very intelligent woman and I hope for further contact.

Saturday, 9 June
This morning we left for the shrine of Sidi Bou Khalef. This Moslem saint lived in the neighbourhood of Azigza many years ago having been sent from Arabia to proselytise the Berbers of the Atlas. He settled among them and lived as a shepherd and married a Berber girl. One day, the story goes, a man sought shelter with him from his enemies. When they arrived the saint offered instead his own son, so he was killed and his guest went free. His godly life resulted in his name becoming honoured. Our guide is a pleasant man named Lahacen. We took the path beyond his village and went on round the curve of the hill—across the river to the village of Zaweet. Old Fakeeh Omar came out to greet us with his ancient, incredibly dusty spectacles on the tip of his nose and his one large front tooth commanding the scene. Kaye told him we would return in an hour, as she wanted to visit the gorge. This is beyond the shrine of Si Bou Khalef and gaunt crags dip down into the river in places so that we had to wade through. On our return we entered the fakeeh's house and soon had an audience of eight men. They denied the death of Christ so I suggested that we use the brains God had given us and examine our differences of opinion. They liked that idea and agreed to listen as well as shout! When we had finished two of the men followed at a distance and then asked for our teaching on divorce, so I took out my Bible and had another quarter of an hour with them. It was a most encouraging time and I overheard one man, a fakeeh, saying to another, 'This word hits me like an iron...'

Sunday, 10 June
This evening the wife of the soldier I talked to on the roof gave birth to a baby. Kaye delivered her and one of the women ran onto the roof and gave the joy-cry, turning in the direction of the village so that everyone knew. A birth on our last day had to be a good sign!

Monday, 11 June
We left early this morning for the long journey back to Demnate. Lilla Fatima lent us mules and packed us up some bread, chicken and eggs. But we had a half-wit for a guide!
He twice let the mules bolt while we were walking and I was so tired that I fell soundly asleep while he was searching for them. It was a terrific climb up over the Tizi to Tamadour and a rocky, wearying way down to Ait Chitachen. We found much mauve and white hibiscus growing in the woods on the way down. At the bottom, by the river Gzef the oleander was out in full, glorious bloom. We crossed the river not far from where, ten years earlier, I had camped with the Bishop and Si Mohammed when boar hunting. Most of the way back I walked, dragging the very mulish mule behind me for fear he would bolt again. Our unperturbed guide disappeared entirely for an hour or so and when, on his appearance, I enquired whether or not he was supposed to look after the beasts he replied that he had felt so tired that he sat for a while by the wayside. A quite reasonable attitude I suppose! When I suggested jokingly that perhaps he should ride—he did quite happily—while we more or less staggered the last steps.

This interesting extract tells of places and people encountered by Swannie that could not easily have been so well-described by another. In it we feel the depth of her compassion for the Berber people and her interest in their history as well as their culture. The two verses below are part of the poem mentioned earlier and one of many inspirational poems Swannie had later compiled into a booklet entitled *Along the Way.*

Little Daisy

Hi little daisy, growing by the wayside,
Have you got a bed for a weary little fly?
Said the little daisy growing by the wayside,
'Yes, poor thing, you needn't pass me by.
There's a cosy little bed
Though it's only on my head
And you're really very welcome for the night.'
So like all his brother flies
He just closed his hundred eyes,
And slept until the morning light.

Hi little daisy, growing by the wayside,
Do you have a word for a mortal passing by?
Said the little daisy growing by the wayside,
'Why not take a lesson from the fly?
If he finds such comforts free
In a little flower like me,
Don't you think that God, who loves you more than flies,
To your smallest care gives heed and meets your every need?
Let my carefree little guest make you wise.'

Chapter 9
The Start of Berber Radio

BY THE SUMMER OF 1966 SWANNIE had begun the preparation of Scriptures for use in the Berber radio programmes in earnest and some of the boys she had taught were able to help her. It is not safe to give names as there is still much persecution of Christians in Morocco. If a name is mentioned it is a popular first name and not easily connected to any one person.

Instead of Meknes, Swannie now lived in a chalet in Ain Jabou, a little village nearer the Middle Atlas Mountains. She loved the clear mountain air and the privacy of her little home there, as well as its accessibility for visits to the Berber mountain people. It was necessary to check her translation for authenticity as well as correctness of pronunciation so she asked an old friend whom she had known when she lived in Mijjot whether he would be able to visit each day and help her with this. He readily agreed and it was decided that his young son, Mohammed, should also come to the chalet. Together they listened intently and checked the New Testament passages

Swannie read out to them.

Throughout the summer months of 1966 they worked hard together until suddenly, one very hot day in August, young Mohammed started to feel unwell. It was not long before he was running a high fever and Swannie was so concerned that she asked his father if she could send for an ambulance to take him into hospital. But his parents still held many of the old Berber superstitions ingrained in their memories and they had a great fear that the young boy might die while in hospital and his body would not be returned to them.

By the third day Mohammed was unconscious and it was quite obvious to Swannie that there would be no chance of recovery unless something radical was done. She pleaded again for permission to send for an ambulance. The distraught parents eventually gave their consent after Swannie had given a firm promise that she would be personally responsible for bringing the boy back to them. When the ambulance arrived she and the father travelled with him to the hospital which was thirty miles away. The boy was very sick and for ten days lay in a desperate condition. He was given the treatment needed and every night Swannie watched over him. Friends and colleagues all over the country had been informed of the situation and were praying for the young lad's recovery day and night. Gradually he began to recover and by the end of August the doctor was able to pronounce him fit enough to leave hospital provided he was taken somewhere suitable to rest and convalesce. Swannie promised immediately that she would take him home to her little chalet where he would be given plenty of good food and recuperate quickly in the fresh mountain air.

It was a great day of rejoicing when Mohammed, wearing dark glasses and a straw hat to protect his eyes and head, arrived back home with his father and Swannie. The small village community had considered him already dead when he was taken away in the ambulance and were amazed at such a recovery. The little boy gained strength daily and was soon walking with Swannie into the mountains. As he gained strength Mohammed would contentedly walk beside Swannie, holding her hand or guiding the mule that she was riding. Mohammed became very close to her heart. So much so that she wrote in her diary that he was 'her spiritual son.' What a vulnerable, tender-hearted woman Swannie was underneath the sometimes prim and serious exterior.

The remainder of that summer passed quickly, Swannie making sure that Mohammed received all the convalescent care he needed. But the hectic, hot weather and the extra work involved was taking its toll on her own health. In October she had to be admitted to the same hospital in Tangier with a rare form of meningitis. The enforced hospital stay seems to have been a blessing in disguise as Swannie there met up again with Harry Ratcliffe, a missionary from the High Atlas Mountains who was extremely fluent in a different Berber dialect than herself. He was interested in setting up some Berber radio programmes and together they were able to discuss the possibility of a combined radio programme in the two respective dialects.

In 1968 Swannie was due to go to America on deputation work but before leaving she recorded 52 messages with Harry Ratcliffe in the two different Berber tongues. Everything was complete and the messages ready to send off to Trans World Radio for transmission when suddenly, at the last minute and as she was having a shower, Swannie had a horrifying thought. Was the music they had used in the programme copyright? They had not obtained permission to use it and, rushing immediately to look at the label, she discovered it was!

Devastated she phoned Harry Ratcliffe. He was living in Tangier and she dashed up in a friend's car to collect him before travelling again to Malaga and recording the messages for a second time. By some mistake, or miracle, the first recordings had been sent by slow mail to Trans World Radio and as the second set were sent by airmail they arrived first. Calamity was avoided but Swannie never forgot the lesson she learned—check, check and check again was to become her motto. We can imagine Swannie's feelings when on 8th February 1969 at 10.30 p.m. medium-wave the first Berber broadcast was transmitted from Monte Carlo Trans World Radio. All the hard work seemed worthwhile when she heard her own voice telling out for the first time on radio the gospel message in the Shilha tongue.

But clouds had been gathering darkly over Morocco for several years and in May 1967 some of the G.M.U. workers were officially asked to leave the country. For a long time it had been felt hat the radio work in Meknes would have to cease and that this particular ministry could be carried out just as effectively in a country that was more open to the gospel than Morocco was at that time. After much consideration suitable buildings were bought in Malaga, Spain, where there were facilities for future expansion as well as the present needs. A print shop, later to become known as the Christian Media Centre, was set up and is still very much in operation.

Swannie was one of the last missionaries to leave Morocco. Before she left at the end of 1969 a suitable country had to be found where she could give her undivided attention to producing radio messages with her Berber helpers. But the men would need other work in order to support themselves and send money back home to their families still in Morocco. The recording studio was now working well in Malaga and it was proposed that Swannie should go there to do the recording at three-monthly intervals. But a place in a country not too far away from Malaga was needed where Swannie and her co-workers could base.

The arranged months were spent by Swannie in deputation work in the States and then she made a short visit to England. Still nothing was on the agenda and she was by then expecting to be moved out of Morocco at any time. It was not until the final warning came for her to leave the country or she would be expelled permanently, that the needed guidance arrived. Swannie met a Berber man who had returned home to visit his family. He had found work in Corsica and informed her that there was plenty of work available on the farms and in the vineyards there. She immediately went into action and contacted a French pastor living in Corsica, Monsieur Guyot, to find out the authenticity of the Berber man's report and the possibility of obtaining work permits for the men. Then she made the first of many visits she was to make to Corsica during the following ten years, this time for the sole purpose of being introduced to farmers who would take on Moroccan workers and find out if suitable accommodation was available for the men.

Swannie's first trip was made by boat from Tangier to Genoa and then on to Bastia in Northern Corsica. From there she took the little train through wild but beautiful countryside to Ajaccio, where she was met by Mons. Guyot and his wife. As they talked together and discussed arrangements with the farmers she marvelled again at God's provision. Swannie was about to enter yet another dangerous stage of her eventful life.

1932 Swannie aged 22 and,
in her own words:
'Just Born Again!'

S.S. 'BALTROVER' In 1944 Swannie sailed for Morocco on this ship. The second world war was in full progress and it was one of a convoy military ships.

S.S. " BALTROVER."

1948. Swannie in front of her first home alongside the Atlas Berbers – a little yellow tent!

December 1950. Swannie beside the mud and thatch nuella that was built for her by Berber friends. Her first-ever own home was on the Middle Atlas Mountains.

A drawing,done by Swannie
herself, of Aberbash, a good friend
from early years in Morocco.

1952. Swannie outside her nuella with
two Berber friends. An English woman
on a motor bike caused much comment!

Ain Jahu 1966. Swannie and Mohamed
outside her chalet. The young boy had
just recovered,,,,,, from meningitis.

1967.   Swannie in Meknes with some of her G.M.U. colleagues.

1967 Swannie in one of the places she loved best. With Berber friends among their tents near Meknes.

Hafdaoui and friend Omar sharing a meal with friends. All eating from one plate in the centre of the floor was a Berber custom to which Swannie quickly adjusted.

The Haven, another children's home in Azrou, Morocco.

1976   Swannie with her Berber co-worker in translation and radio work.   With his wife and young daughter at the Radio Station in Malaga.

A young Berber girl washes the hands of Gordon McCrostie, a colleague of Swannie, before the start of a meal up at her mountain home.

Swannie's ashes were taken to Morocco by colleagues and spread round the cedar trees she loved so much.   The monkey- one of a special species to be found in that area of Morocco, seems to have also taken a liking for that particularl spot.

Chapter 10
Life at the Inn

ON 27TH JULY THE LITTLE TRAIN from Bastia ploughed its way through the rugged scenery of Northern Corsica to Ajacio. In her diary for that date Swannie writes:

I was met at the station by a Mr. and Mrs. Guyot and am now up in the hills above Ajaccio in the loveliest little chalet. Best of all I was introduced to an Algerian farmer who will give me contracts of work for the men.

Swannie then returned to Morocco with the good news. She went to Bastia and checked the time of her boat to Genoa but there was such a dreadful wind and that she struggled even to carry her case to the port. It was a tortuous journey as the sea was very rough and Swannie heaved a sigh of relief when she was safely back in Morocco.

The three men who had agreed to go with Swannie to Corsica were friends of long standing. She taught them to read when they were young boys and they, in return, had been only too willing as they grew into young men to help her with the Shilha tongue. They were delighted with the news that work and suitable accommodation had been found as times were hard in Morocco and they needed to help their families as well as support Swannie in the radio work she was doing. Shilha was the dialect of the Middle Mountain Berbers and although Swannie was able to speak the language quite proficiently, she was adamant that a native Berber must first check any message before it was recorded in Malaga.

So arrangements for the move were made but it was a long process. Getting papers signed and passports released was not easy in Morocco and very often bribes were offered to speed up the delays. But Swannie told the men in no uncertain terms that God was capable of getting them into Corsica without any bribes!

After long weeks of waiting there came news that the precious documents were ready in Casablanca. Swannie went to collect them and found to her dismay that there was only one passport—suspense until the end. But all was well and the men beamed with delight when their official papers were placed into their hands. But all is delay in Morocco and when the men went to have their medicals they were told to return for the results in the afternoon—the X-Ray had broken down.

By November 20th all was cleared and the men went off in high spirits to buy provisions for the journey. Then they were packed into a goods train and taken to Tangier where they boarded a boat for Corsica. This time Swannie left by air so that she would be able to meet the men when they arrived. Again we take a look at Swannie's diary:

November 24th 1969

I took the train to Bastia at 2.30 p.m. and put up at a hotel for the night. Next day I went down to the port while it was still dark and saw the boat appearing. Oh, the joy to see the three men coming down the gangway, looking well in spite of their long journey. We ran up the High Street and just caught the little train to Ajaccio. After a good meal the men were taken to meet their employer, Mr. Perretti.

November 26th

The men spent the day in the village of Pila Canale after Mr. Perretti had taken them to see their new quarters. I stayed in the village with a nurse, Mlle. Bozzi, who was very helpful. There is something sinister about this village at night; no lights at all in the streets, wild mountains all around and the tall houses dark and eerie.

November 30th

Today I went to see the men. They have the loneliest little stone house in the most lovely scenery, wild but beautiful. Next day I was invited to drink coffee with Mr. and Mrs. Perretti.

November 30th

This morning I walked the lonely way to the men's house but there was trouble. Allal and Drees, who have never quarrelled much before, were in combat over some lost sheep. I talked to them, telling them what harm could be done by such quarrelling and in the end Allal went over to Drees and asked his pardon.

December 2nd

Went to see the men, taking a football, some books, tea, chestnuts, a cabbage and some sheep fat. Also some photographs of their families that I had taken before leaving Morocco. In the evening Drees came and worked with me, checking the messages for the Berber radio which I had done.

December 8th

I have found a nice little room at the inn and will be a 'pensionnaire' at 500 francs monthly. The relief to have a room of my own where I can study and invite people in! The time has come to return to Malaga to record the Berber messages. I will leave tomorrow.

December 20th

Started my journey back to Corsica. One of the men from the radio station took me to the airport but there was a fog over Madrid so the plane was delayed for 2 hours. We circled the airport but had to return to Malaga. Finally got the plane to Nice via Madrid—but what a journey! The plane I took was scheduled to stop at Barcelona before continuing on to Nice but we were all told to leave the plane in order to pass police formalities. No one seemed to know what we were supposed to do. The Nice travellers were put together and left in the hall until an official remembered us and came back in great haste to escort us the length of the building to a certain desk to get our boarding cards. It was then I discovered that my ticket was not in my bag! With my full handbag, briefcase of Berber programmes, typewriter and coat I fled back as fast as I could, while in the distance I could dismally hear my flight number being called. The first official I met knew no English and was useless, but he directed me to a desk where a girl spoke English and gave me the sweetest smile saying, 'But, Madame, your flight is just taking off!' A sympathetic man at the desk took to his heels and about seven minutes later returned with my ticket, directing me to the end of the hall to pass the usual formalities. I staggered off again and got my boarding card and was directed to the gate. As I fled through this a little official grabbed me and demanded airport tax. I told him that my plane was about to go but he could not have cared less. Just then a little man with a bald head and spectacles turned and told the official that he would pay my tax. Again I passed through the gate but this time the police grabbed me and demanded my passport. He took a long time to go through it and finally returned it to me with a glare. I was so thankful to board that plane that I only died 99 of the 100 deaths I usually do when flying.

At Nice I went to see if there was a seat on the plane to Ajaccio. The very friendly official said he would not know until ten minutes before takeoff, but to have my baggage ready. I went to collect my two cases and found that only one was there. On enquiring the reason I was told that they did not know why—it

98

was very unfortunate but the case was probably in Madrid, Malaga or Barcelona! Since all my irreplaceable Berber books were in this case, also papers, camera, binoculars and Christmas presents for the men, you can imagine that I felt more than a little sad. However, I was told to return to the desk at 4 p.m. and, praise God who saw that I could cope with no more, I was given a seat. The Guyots met me at Ajaccio and took me to the home of the Poglianos, where I spent the night.

December 24th—Christmas Eve
Changed my traveller's cheques and boarded the bus to the village of Pila Canale. At dusk we arrived at the little inn that is a short way out of the village of Pila Canale. I was shown to my little room up some stairs behind the inn and at 8 p.m. went down to supper. The dining room is a tiny place and opens into the kitchen where the family eat.

Christmas Day 1969
I was the only one at breakfast but one of the little old ladies sat me by a log fire in the kitchen and game me a large basin of coffee and a lump of dry bread, also a saucer of jam.
I really enjoyed this strange Christmas fare. Then with my Arabic Bible and a new very large, coloured umbrella, which I had managed to buy for the men, I set off for the little house in the hills. The frost was still on the path and thin ice was over the puddles. But the sun was shining and the various green colours of the maquis (moors) were rich and beautiful against the blue of the mountains, by now snow-capped. I was feeling just a little sorry for myself, to have begun the day with only one old lady I didn't know and my family and friends far away, when I felt a sudden thrill. Had not I arrived on Christmas Eve at a little wayside inn just as Someone Else had done? I could have danced for joy at the thought of such a privilege and regretted only that I had no gifts to bring, not even the chicken that I had promised the men. I found them working on the hillside thinking I had been delayed and you can imagine our mutual joy. We were just going to settle down to

our menu of potatoes and onions in tomato sauce when along the track came Mr. Perretti in his pickup van. He told Said to slaughter one of his five big chickens and gave us some loaves of bread to eat with it. The men killed and plucked the chicken and we made a good tajin (a Moroccan stew). We had our service together and prayed that my case with all its precious contents would somehow be brought back to me, whatever country it arrived in. I started back with Allal about 4.30 p.m. leaving Drees and Said to collect and milk the sheep. When we entered the inn the old lady told us that a man from Ajaccio had called and left me something. There, sitting safely in the corner, was my lost suitcase. Nothing was missing although it was not locked. So Allal took back the gifts and photographs and the men enjoyed them on Christmas Day after all. It had been a wonderful Christmas Day after all.

Swannie's first days in Corsica were unlike any that she had ever experienced before. Her time at the inn was different from any other period in her life. Never before had she lived in a shabby little room behind the general stores eater whatever could be cooked in a large saucepan on a tiny gas ring in the kitchen. She was intrigued by the food that was served! The liquid was invariably drained off whatever it was in the saucepan and called 'soup.' If this looked just too anaemic some noodles were added then whatever had sunk to the bottom was next ladled out. Sometimes little bits of tripe and carrots or a bit of boiled beef, or once even 'a pitiful little sparrows with long necks and wobbly heads that stared up at me from sightless eye sockets as if to ask pardon for its skinny body.' Sometimes vegetables were dished out of the same saucepan as a third course with olive oil poured over these. Now and again there was fresh fish or a tiny piece of meat and dessert was always yoghurt with an apple or dried figs.

Breakfast was eaten in solitary style between the fireplace and the kitchen sink and consisted of a lump of dry bread and jam and a basin of coffee. But Swannie kept very well on her frugal diet and had no complaints despite its monotony.

In the evening it was livelier in the inn than at midday. There were often visitors and the wine flowed profusely. Very often one of the guests would indulge too freely and make themselves impossible for Swannie to tolerate. On one occasion she wrote to a friend that

> *...two nights ago the village postman—a young fellow from Paris—really had too much to drink and was insupportable. So I removed myself into the kitchen with my apple and with very quiet dignity told him that he positively wearied me....*

Those of us who knew Swannie can well understand how humiliated the young man was made to feel. If he did appear the next evening he would be much more subdued.

The washroom facilities were probably the hardest thing for Swannie to cope with. Both toilet and washbasin were outside and she had to pluck up courage to face the bitter weather and freezing cold water. To make matters worse for her the door had swollen and wouldn't shut. She writes '...habit drives me to take the risk of a shower and so far I have not caught pneumonia nor had to cope with Peeping Toms.'

Sunday was Swannie's special day and whatever the weather she never missed making the arduous journey up the maquis to the lonely homestead where the men lived. She would arrive early in the morning and eat with the men then they would get down to the hours of what she called the 'eternal business' of checking every word she was to use in the Berber broadcasts she was composing. In Swannie's opinion it was essential that every word be checked and every sentence approved by the Berber men and pronounced to their satisfaction. For this work the men needed to be at peace with one another but often the wet days were wearisome for them. They tired of each other's company as they were cooped up together for long hours and even days at a time when work outside was impossible and this caused irritation. Only once a month when a small community of French Christians came in from Ajaccio to Mlle. Bozzi's house did they venture out and meet others. But Swannie noted how little they complained considering the circumstances and the differences in temperament.

The inn was Swannie's first home in Corsica and her own creative mind renamed the place 'Bethany.' The simple reason for this being the proprietors, two little old sisters and a brother, who reminded her of Mary, Martha and Lazarus from the story she knew so well in the Bible. All three of them were unmarried and the sisters were perfect replicas, so Swannie thought, of Mary and Martha in their old age. The elder sister never stopped working; a tiny woman with white hair screwed up in a little knob at the back of her head with thick woollen stockings that always concertined down her skinny legs. But she had the sweetest smile as she served in the shop, cooked for the pensionnaires and carried great logs along the road for the fire. She and was first to rise and the last to go to bed. Her sister was also white-haired but quite different. She had a perm, pulled her stockings up straight and was usually found sitting by the fire, not even noticing any chaos around her. When Swannie appeared she was always eager to sit and talk and seemed very attracted to spiritual matters. The little brother 'Lazarus' had an expression of continual bewilderment and kept twitching. Swannie had to keep a tight rein on her imagination or she would find herself forgetting which century she was in and begin to attribute his peculiarities to the unpleasant experience of being dead for four days!

So Swannie's first experiences in Corsica came when she was sheltering in a little room at the inn. Soon she was to move on to more suitable accommodation but never, through the long and often lonely years to come, did she ever forget the stay in her personal 'Bethany.'

Chapter 11
Operation Corsica

THE FIRST FEW WEEKS IN CORSICA were exciting for both Swannie and her fellow workers. Everything was new and there was a sense of the unknown that at first lent an enchantment to each day.

Sunday was still a happy day, for Swannie would invariably go out early and make her way through the solitude of the wild woodland to visit her friends in the hut that was their makeshift home. The scenery was beautiful and very pleasant in good weather but during the wet days it was hard walking for Swannie. When work was impossible and the men were 'caged in,' Swannie found herself often wondering how they could stand it. She would arrive about 10 a.m. with provisions for making a good meal and together they would fellowship and rest. They did little complaining and were no doubt much encouraged by Swannie's visits and the delicious chicken she would cook for them on tiny stove.

But there was much work to be done and it soon became apparent to Swannie that the men's crowded quarters and close proximity were doing nothing to help their Moroccan tempers—which were becoming more and more frayed. She must find a place to live where it would be more convenient for the men to visit her. When she had a place of her own she could sort out a work programme to suit them all and help the men escape the close confines of their surroundings. In March 1970 Number 1, Rue Pierre Bonardi became available. It was a small apartment situated down near the port in Ajaccio and enabled the men to come in by bus from Pila Canale on their free day and give time to checking the scripts that Swannie had completed during the week. She was able to cook the three men a meal as they worked, which was very much enjoyed, and a lot of work was accomplished. It was more private than the room at the inn and Swannie was pleased with the move. But she often waited in vain for the men to arrive and at such times her patience was sorely tried, although she was always very appreciative of the time given by the three Berber men. In one of her letters home she writes:

How little listeners realise how much is involved in the making of these radio programmes. As far as my part of the translation work is concerned the Berber men are an essential—I feel it to be quite imperative that they approve every sentence and every word pronounced to their satisfaction. For this work the men need to be at peace with each other and have a right attitude. How can this programme escape the warfare?

It didn't! The first time she was due to go to Malaga to record her scripts, Swannie felt sure they needed a final check. She waited several days for one of the men to arrive and when Drees walked into her apartment she cried on his shoulder with relief. Her treatment of the work was very professional and the first Easter in Corsica found Swannie on her way back to Malaga to record the broadcasts she had completed on time.

By the summer of 1970 Swannie was feeling much the

worse for wear and longed for some friends and encouragement. It had been a hard year and she decided to make a trip home to visit friends in England and take up the kind offer of a trip to Scotland, in the hope that the fresh air and good food would improve her health. She loved Scotland and very much enjoyed the trip, returning south feeling much better. But back there she was taken ill with a sudden attack of shingles and was still in a weak condition when the time came for her to return to Corsica. She travelled by train and then by sea and back at last in her apartment on the island she wrote in her diary:

> *I am sitting in my little studio again by the light of my branch lamp. It is as though I have never been away, except that my back aches, a continual reminder of the last few weeks of shingles! I wait anxiously for Drees to come.*

Then later;

> *He has not come so I will have my meal. I was up early to prepare the tajin (stew) and was hoping to share it with him. This stalemate of my work is most serious—for that is why I am here in Corsica. I have to admit that I sometimes get sick with the strain!*

When asked by the man who was to employ Hussein if she would meet the young Berber and let him rest in her home until he was able to be picked up, Swannie was delighted. She rose about 5 a.m. in order to be at the port when the boat arrived. She records:

> *It is strangely quiet in the port at this time of morning, but so much nicer than in the noisy daytime. I sat on the wall and watched the little pilot boat go out to meet the 'Napolean.' The Ramadan moon hung high over the gulf and the morning star*

twinkled brightly over the ridge of mountains on the other side. Like a fairy palace the 'Napolean' came in sight. I didn't see Hussein on deck so I went to the staircase down which the passengers disembarked. When he saw me he gave a joyful cry of 'Miss Swan,' then rushed and kissed me on both cheeks shouting, 'She comes from Meknes!' Immediately a crowd of poor lost voyagers pulled out their contracts and surrounded me, imploring me to tell them where to go, as none of them had been met. I got the dear fellow to my studio and gave him hot coffee and bread and jam. Then I covered my bed as he was rather travel-soiled, and left him to sleep until his boss called for him about 5 p.m. Now Hussein is here I am going every weekend to Pila Canale and will have a meeting with them all. Poor Hussein—he is alone in a little house about 7 kilometres from the others.

Soon Swannie's second Christmas in Corsica arrived and again she could write in her diary that it had been wonderful. In the afternoon she had been able to show her film of the Christmas story to a family of Arabs, then went back home to prepare tea for the (now) four Berbers from Pila Canale. In the evening they went to the home of the men's boss, Mon. Pogliano, and enjoyed a big Moroccan stew. Two Berber men from the Riff tribe joined them and Swannie was able to speak again about God's love and the Christmas story. The next night she made a visit to the village inn and again had the opportunity to talk, this time with Corsicans who were staying there. She asked for a French Bible and was able to answer their questions from it in their own language.

Once into 1971 things began to get more difficult. News from the families back in Morocco was disturbing to some of the men and that, combined with the bad weather and restricted living conditions, encouraged many quarrels among them. Swannie continued to go out every weekend to help resolve difficulties and share what food she had, but their hut was not heated and she began to get severe rheumatic pains.

After the first few weeks of awful homesickness Hussein was settling down well and was always praising God for His goodness. All alone in his lodging and not able to cook, he never made any complaints and people often commented on his cheery, shining face. But Drees and Said were fast becoming discouraged and Allal was reacting badly to the injustices they felt they were receiving. Their employer refused to pay their insurance and yet expected them to drive the tractor without any suitable cover. Without insurance papers it would be impossible to renew passports and the men were talking of leaving at the end of February. Swannie's radio programme was suffering under the extreme pressure and she writes in a letter to a friend in England:

This is my darkest hour so far and the situation grows steadily worse. As yet the men are still together but only in bodily presence it seems. Drees and Said have said they can no longer work with Allal, who is spending many of his nights with Arab youths who drink in the village. But I will talk to him....

Later she writes:

I went out to the little cabin when I knew Allal was alone. The door was shut and I knocked and pushed it open. It was almost dark and very dirty. Allal was lying under his blankets in a corner. I told him to get up and light a fire, which he did. Then we sat down to talk. Before many minutes he exploded! It was not the Allal I knew from Meknes speaking. His face was contorted with anger and insane frustration. It was not difficult now to believe that he had lifted a hatchet to attack one of the other men, as they had said. I know the Berber rage having witnessed it several times when I lived amongst them in Morocco. It was no good talking so I just sat and let his misery run out. Then suddenly he apologised for his outburst and, saying his head hurt, rolled back onto his bed. He remained there for a long time, refusing to eat when the

*others came back. But he listened when I read to them and after
I had prayed I was surprised to hear a clear Amen from him. I
believe the head injury he had in a road accident in Morocco is
partly to blame and, being a sociable fellow, the loneliness of the
moor has not helped. He has sought relief with bad company.*

Swannie was devastated at the turn of events and looked back in her diary for 1969, where she had written a daily account of her contact with Allal and the others before moving into Corsica. She was convinced that she had followed the right guidance step by step and wondered where she had gone wrong. She was utterly exhausted, but was given a strong assurance that God had led her and the men to Corsica and that He would not fail them. But these times were not easy.

It was then that Swannie decided to write her first article about Corsica for the G.M.U. Until then she had kept silent and the work was hardly mentioned but she felt that, before her next deputation trip to America, she should bring supporters up to date with the special vision she had. This was that a restaurant and club room might be set up where Arabs and Berbers could meet, have coffee and a place to talk our their problems. Other helpers would be needed for such a project and Swannie wanted to be able to talk more fully about this on her proposed trip to the U.S.A. later in the year with a view to obtaining more support.

The article for the magazine had been written before the episode with Allal took place and was due to be published in the March issue. It looked to Swannie at that time as though the article might be a mockery of how the work was really progressing. So when Allal came to her later and said he would be leaving at the end of the month, she made no effort to hold him back. There were bitter lessons she felt he needed to learn if he were ever to be used in helping with the radio and translation work again.

In February 1971 there was thick snow in Ajaccio. Drees

THE TOUCH OF LOVE

continued to visit Swannie but she was seldom able to get out to see the other men in Pila Canale. Drees would often have to stay the night and he was a morose and silent companion, though always helpful with the language and eager to suggest improvements in the programmes. He was loathe to have his voice heard on the air because of fear of reprisal in Morocco when he went back later in the year for the wedding feast of his father. He was frightened that he would be thrown into prison if his voice were heard propagating the Christian message on the radio. Swannie understood his fear and did not press him, recognising the fact that just then he was unable to face the persecution he would certainly meet.

In the middle of March they travelled together to Malaga and her diary reveals just what a rough crossing they had:

The problem is to know whether the devil is having a last fling at us or the Lord testing me a little longer! We managed to sleep stretched out on the seats of an empty coach all night on the train from Marseilles to Barcelona but the last train was held up outside the station for half an hour so we lost the connection to Madrid. There was one two hours later but this arrived five minutes after our train for Malaga left. This meant we would have to sit all night in the station or pay for a hotel, and money is running out. Travelling is getting more and more difficult but still we do not have what St. Paul suffered—shipwreck, stoning and imprisonment. Poor Drees—no one can say he makes good company! He speaks only when spoken to and looks sad and troubled all the time. Yet for the radio work he is the one that has made it all possible because for in that respect he is efficient and reliable. We both longed for somewhere to stretch out as we had been sitting around all day when a man at the station offered to take us to a cheap hotel. So we went with him. To my dismay a young lady led us to a small room with two beds. I said this would not do at all—so we were out on the street once more and by this time it was midnight! We tried three more hotels and they were full. At last we went back to the station and I went up to a group

109

of officials and demonstrated my need to sleep, showing them our train tickets. One of them had his heart touched and wrote 127 on a paper and gave it to me. When I pointed to Drees he wrote 246, then took my suitcase and off we went down a narrow street where he took out a key and opened some great iron doors. We went through a small court, up three flights of stairs and into an apartment. We were shown two rooms—no oilcloth or mat just wooden boards, no hot water but a clean bed in each room. When I got into bed it was so cold that I feared for my sciatica but I was so tired that I slept until 6 a.m. When the kind officials came with our passports I paid him 246 pesetas and we started another day of travelling. Tonight we should get a meal and a hot bath but just now we have had lunch—a half apple and dry bread that I bought last Thursday in Corsica! We arrived in Malaga much later than planned and so no one was there to meet us as they had met the earlier train. But we took a taxi with the very last of my money and today we are recording. To my astonishment Drees suddenly announced in the studio that he would make the radio announcements. I was speechless but got up and he sat before the microphone, speaking into it without a moment's hesitation.

The above entry in Swannie's diary gives some indication as to the difficulties she experienced in translating the radio broadcasts into the Shilha tongue and recording them in Malaga. Her health was bad at this time as she was suffering from bronchitis as well as sciatica and it must be remembered that she was by that time sixty-one years old. Perhaps not the ideal age for such a hazardous task, some might say, but it was the path Swannie felt she must take and she never deviated from it.

There was good news awaiting them on their return to Corsica. Drees had been offered work in a nursery above Ajaccio and better living quarters were provided. He would share an apartment with four young men, all Arabs. Perhaps life in Corsica was about to improve for Drees!

Chapter 12
Morocco Again—Then America

SWANNIE, SUFFERING FROM ACUTE RHEUMATIC PAINS, was recovering from what she called a 'dark period' by the end of 1971. She was a talented poet and during the hard times tended to pour out her heart in verse. In later years her dear friend Jenny Wilberforce, who was always so supportive of Swannie, helped her gather the poems together and have them printed in a very acceptable book form. Some of the poems were written during Swannie's young, carefree days in her homeland, England. Others during her years in Morocco, the foreign land she always called home, and the latter ones in Corsica. Swannie's writing always portrayed clearly the depth of her emotions at a given time and gives a clear insight into her personality. Often she would do one of her own sketches to portray what she had written. The poems are beautiful to read and there are still a few copies of the booklet available.

In the summer of 1971 Swannie had been able to have a holiday in Switzerland when friends kindly loaned her their chalet for a week or so. Jenny and another friend from England joined her and they all felt better in each other's company and had lively and sometimes hilarious conversations. It was a time of particular encouragement for Swannie and the sunshine and fresh air proved a great tonic and prepared her for the coming busy months. She planned to travel to Malaga after Switzerland to do some recording, then needed to return to Corsica before making a brief visit to Morocco. It was possible for Swannie to do this because when the missionaries had been asked to leave Morocco it was on the agreement that they could make return visits, but only for a period of three months at a time. Many of the G.M.U. workers took the opportunity of taking the trip periodically in order to meet up with Moroccan friends who were continuing in the church there, although it was not an open witness. The underground church there has survived and remained active right until this present time.

Swannie was eager to go to Morocco, not only to visit friends but because she had promised a young Berber woman, Ito, that she would try and find her parents who lived in the High Atlas. Ito was a young girl whom she had known some years before in Meknes. She had been a member of Swannie's group of girls at one time but her parents had disapproved and made her leave. She had married and now lived with her husband in Corsica. Itto's parents had been very poor and living in desperate conditions in Meknes and now lived in even more poverty on the mountains. Itto was very upset because there was no way she could get help to them as her husband would not help. She was desperate to keep in touch with her family and try to send them some money. Swannie wanted the opportunity to keep her promise and try to find the family before her next deputation visit to the States. So October found Swannie once again among her beloved Berber friends but this time she had made preparations for the hazardous journey by having a cholera injection in Malaga.

There were severe after-effects and by the time she arrived

in Tangier, Swannie was feeling exhausted even before her proposed trip started. So she rested for a couple of days before taking the train out to her old home in Meknes.

There she had the privilege of meeting again with Omar, the son of her old friend Ben Ashir. She was also able to visit the wives of some of the men working out in Corsica. The men were all sending money back to Morocco in order to provide for their families, indeed Allal had returned home and married a young Berber girl. Swannie was delighted to see him settled down so comfortably in the house he had built for his family and parents with money he had saved from his time in Corsica. The family were so happy to be together and in comparative luxury after suffering poverty for many years. It was a great relief for Swannie to know that the movement of the men to Corsica from Morocco had proved beneficial to the families as well as herself. She was glad to be able to reassure Allal's wife that though he would return very soon to Corsica, he would make regular trips back home to the family.

Swannie also made a trip out to the orphanage at Ain Leuh to see her two missionary friends who were still faithfully working there, despite their age. She shared a wonderful dinner with the children, many she had known in past years and now looked so grown up. She was particularly delighted to meet Aberbash again, a handsome young man now though only a boy when Swannie taught him, and now working full time at the orphanage.

Aberbash was very interested to hear about Itto and Swannie's plans to look for her family in the mountains. He said she needed a travelling companion as the way was dangerous for a woman on her own. When he asked if it would be possible for him to go with her Swannie said she would be delighted to accept. So it was decided that he would accompany her and on 16th October the two started off on their long journey into the High Atlas. The following is an extract from Swannie's diary. It is well documented as usual with her colourful descriptions and wry comments:

Here I am sitting by the roadside waiting for a car to Azrou. We are in Khenifra and have been walking since early morning as soon as it was light enough to see the rocky mountain path.

Oh what a night I've had!!! I slept on an earth floor—no bed, no mattress, with five men, one woman, three children and ten thousand times ten thousand skippety, hoppety, hilariously happy and hungry little fleas! Not one small area of my poor body did they leave in peace. We had no covers—just a dirty bit of rug and a filthy cushion for a pillow. I covered this with my jumper so that my face was not resting on the cushion but when I put my torch on there were so many little fellows jumping over the jumper that I was no better off!

One of the five men was Aberbash, who so bravely offered to come with me to hunt for Itto's family. We finished up in the mountains beyond Beni Mellal. We took the coach from Azrou to here yesterday then paid 2500 francs for a taxi to the foothills of the High Atlas. After that we climbed over rocks and through rushing streams for a couple of hours until my stockings were torn to shreds and my body just dust and perspiration. It is still hot here, but at night turns very cold. I'm just longing to get my clothes off and into a bath to get rid of my 'visitors' but there is a long way to go yet. But it has been worth it! I talked to Itto's family last night in Shilha and they listened intently.

At 2 a.m. I could lie no longer in such torment. I thought of others who had endured such greater torment and tried to praise God, but my praises kept turning into petitions that He put me to sleep. But sleep I could not so I crept over the snoring bodies and sat outside where I found Aberbash also had fled from the tormenting fleas. There, in the sky above, and beautiful beyond words, hung Orion, my favourite constellation. Then I really praised God and for a short time forgot about my poor, afflicted flesh. But it was too cold to stay outside for long so I went in again and offered myself up for second helpings. My little guests didn't waste a moment before accepting! At 3 a.m. I heard the mother go outside and then some rhythmic beating began. Itto had told me that she thought her mother was demon possessed and was preparing herself for a bout. I crept outside and peeped into the tiny hut where she was pounding something in a wooden basin. I asked her what she was doing and she said making coffee to drink! So from 3 a.m. to 5 a.m. I talked with her and the T.B. son who came in to get a light for his keef pipe.

Mission accomplished! I am now on the train returning to Tangier and tomorrow I will be on the boat for Malaga. Have been preparing a tape with slides on 'The History of the Berber Radio' and the move from Morocco to Corsica.
Two more days and I fly to America.

AMERICA 1971–72

Swannie had been looking forward to her American Deputation trip. She had decided to talk about the vision she had for Corsica and try to awaken more interest in that and the Berber radio work.

She had not been to the U.S.A. for some years and this time it seemed like another world! She waited around the airport for some minutes and then the couple who had arranged to meet her, Dr. and Mrs. Francis, arrived and they drove for two hours through Brooklyn and then into New Jersey. The shops were fantastic and Swannie was impressed by the variety and colours in the windows. She had a reputation for always being smartly dressed but was suddenly conscious of her appearance, decided that she was looking a little drab her wardrobe definitely needed 'freshening up.' Perhaps it was time she had a new, more modern look; most of the women seemed to be wearing the new trouser suits and she thought they looked comfortable and attractive at the same time. Very suitable for travelling—perhaps she would buy one and wear it on her way back to

Malaga. It would certainly set a precedent and the missionary wives were sure to love it.

Another thing Swannie noticed, not nearly so pleasant, was that the streets of Brooklyn were nearly empty even though it was barely 6 p.m. This seemed strange to Swannie who had lived so long in the Mediterranean countries where shops were open late into the evening and she wondered why. Later she was told that violence had grown to such an extent that not many people would walk the city streets after dark, certainly not on their own.

From New Jersey Swannie travelled to Ventnor, then on to Ohio to spend Christmas with Lacey Rice, a friend she had worked with in Meknes. She hadn't relished the idea of the long flight she would have to make to reach Lacey's home, but when she arrived she was so glad she had done so. He had a wife and four children and Swannie found them all charming. The prospect of spending Christmas with such a family really cheered her. She was able to relive again with them some of the days spent in Meknes and the time they had travelled up into the Middle Atlas in her jeep with Lacey as chauffeur and Robin, her English friend, as midwife and nurse.

After the months of solitude in Corsica it was so good to be part of a family and again Swannie had an enjoyable Christmas, this time in the heart of the U.S.A. and in a comfortable modern house.

Next stop was Alabama and Swannie found herself again dreading the journey that this time was to be by coach because the fare was so much cheaper. It was a fifteen-hour journey and all she could pray was that it wouldn't be too uncomfortable!

The coach was packed and by the time they reached Cincinnati where they were to change, Swannie was longing to stretch her long legs. The next stop was Louisville and up to then she had not slept at all. However, after the walk about and a meal she fell fast asleep and never even felt uncomfortable. In her diary she wrote: 'It was the Lord. He put me to sleep because I had a meeting next day and needed it!'

It was a strange kind of life for Swannie during those months in America. Often she had to make quick adjustments when she arrived at the different homes where she was to stay. Many of her preconceived ideas had to be changed and she writes again with feeling:

To be truthful and yet give no offence demands so much more tact and wisdom than I had ever realised. It is very wearying!

The itinerary itself was wearing. Between January and May Swannie took meetings in Alabama, Louisiana, Smithville, Colorado, Minneapolis, Chicago and Summit.

In Alabama Swannie found that she was to stay with a young woman who had three children who were all under five years old. Her husband had deserted her the year before and the circumstances were not ideal for a weary missionary. She was able to help the young woman though because the week before, after one of the meetings Swannie had taken, a bearded young man had come up to her and poured out his troubles. His situation was the reverse as his wife had left and taken the children with her. He was devastated and, having seen and tried to understand his grief, Swannie felt in some small way more able to empathise with the young mother. She was realising that the problems people had in America were not much different than those in Morocco or Corsica. It was being there for them when they needed help that mattered.

Swannie did find the weather in America difficult. It changed rapidly and she found herself either wearing too many clothes or not enough. But she was keeping well and as the weeks went by found herself more able to adjust to various kinds of food and different modes of travel, as well as the hours she could sleep or not sleep! From Louisiana Swannie writes:

I am sitting on my bed before breakfast looking out onto the cotton fields where globs of white cotton still stick on their stems. Fifty years roll back and it seems only yesterday that I stood as a little girl before my class at school, holding a clump of raw cotton in my hand and, with all the confidence in the world, giving a lesson on the cotton plant. Now for the first time I can stand in a real cotton plantation, though big, ugly tractors now mostly replace the workers in their brightly coloured clothes. I am staying with some friends who were at the American Base in Sidi Suliman, Morocco. Last night the family and other guests came to see my slides and hear about the radio programme now set up. I go to Smithville next Monday night and have meetings the following day. I will go almost every day to the G.M.U. headquarters and be there for three weeks before flying to Colorado. Then I go by air to California and on to Nebraska, journeys too long for coach so I must fly. My fear of flying makes me ashamed and I continue to pray that it will go.

It was June before Swannie returned to Malaga. After Colorado she had flown to Los Angeles over the Grand Canyon, Utah and the Californian desert. For one who never really overcame her fear of flying the journeying was tremendous. In California on March 18th her diary records:

I spoke in a Sunday school adult class in the morning, then a nursing home, then a church about 45 miles away in the evening. Next morning I was 160 miles south in the desert speaking to a school for boys under court restriction. It was fantastic scenery and very hot. The next evening I was about 250 miles north speaking in a church of converted hippies and Jesus people. This evening I go 25 miles to see a baptism in the sea of some more hippies. On Tuesday I travel day and night and then half a day to Oregon to see the Jessop family who were with me in Morocco. As I go on these long night journeys, sometimes changing in the night and sitting half-doped in bus stations for long hours, I wonder how I am keeping up. But thank God I am!

118

There is an interesting diary selection from Chicago on 18th April:

5.45 a.m. and here I am in the world's most wicked city! Have just had some breakfast after travelling 24 hours in a bus from Thief River Falls, Minnesota. Two big, black cops, flourishing sticks, have just pounced on an evil-looking customer sitting a few tables from me. I had been watching him because he was fixing me with the most evil eye. He really moved when the cops prodded him. It is like being in a gangster film to sit here. The cops are marching round all the time. I shall not get bored while waiting for my bus to Elgin at 7 a.m. I am feeling better than I was two days ago but this is the last time I shall do this tour of the U.S.A. It is too much. At least I've spread the news of the Berber radio programme to hundreds of people by word of mouth, film and last Sunday by radio on a live programme.

I go into Canada at the end of the month and then back to U.S.A.

Then, over the Atlantic, May 30th:
It seems only yesterday I was flying west now I am returning east! I am able to stretch out on the seat as there is no one next to me and I am wearing a trouser suit. It is the usual garment here and I have warned Clem and Dorothea (colleagues in Malaga) that I shall be wearing one. It will give them all a lead or a fright! I am tired in my head but it has been wonderful to have such varied experiences and promote the Berber radio project to so many groups and over so many thousands of miles.

Malaga, May 31st, 7.30 a.m.:
Safe arrival! I watched the dawn over a sea of white, fleecy clouds and it was so beautiful. Clem met me and the plane was an hour late. I will continue my work here while waiting for Drees to come back from Morocco.

Swannie went back to Corsica despite calls from her fellow-workers in Malaga who worried about the isolated and dangerous life she was leading. She was to stay there until 1979 and the next chapter tells us more of events that happened in that wild and beautiful country.

Chapter 13
The 'Wilderness' Years

ON NOVEMBER 1, 1972, SWANNIE WAS able to move into a little one-roomed studio in Ajaccio. It was in the garden of M. Brandon, a French businessman, and his wife. Both were out all day so it was very quiet and to Swannie's delight the window looked out over the mountains.

A more convenient place to live had been needed for some time and it was amazing how Swannie came across the studio. She had searched for days with the French pastor, Mons. Pogliano, for something more suitable. In the agencies in the area even the smallest apartment was costing more than Swannie could afford. Just as it was getting dark and they had almost decided to give up the search they were given the address of a man who had an apartment to rent by the sea. To Swannie's disappointment when they arrived it had already been taken. But the owner, Mr. Brandon, was very helpful and mentioned that he did have a studio flat in his garden that was not usually rented out. If it proved to be adequate for Swannie's needs, then he would let it out to her. They went to

121

look at the studio flat and found it to be quite new and also partly furnished. Mr. Brandon was charging thirty-five pounds per week with everything included. Mons. Pogliano was as surprised as Swannie and assured her that there was nothing to be found at such a price in the entire town. She immediately said she would have it and the owner was so obliging he helped Swannie move her desk and books from the garage where they were stored. She was delighted and writes in her diary:

> *My bed is low and wide and very comfortable. It is so quiet that I feel as if I am alone in the world. I am too far from the town to have students for English (before that Swannie had often taught students to supplement her income) so I must accept the discipline and get on with my radio and translation work.*

Although Swannie was grateful for the little studio flat, she found that after a while the extreme quietness only exaggerated her increasing loneliness. She was experiencing other problems as well as the Corsicans ate a lot of bread which did not suit her health. In a letter Swannie amusingly wrote:

> *I am eating prunes, drinking lots of water and not eating much bread. How I've sighed for All-Bran! Today I had some carrots, olives, beans and a little meat as Drees came. I have meat with him now just on a Sunday as he has a long way to come but I am saving to get him a little second-hand car.*
>
> *Drees is the most faithful, silent, gentle fellow I have met and I still can't get a word out of him except about work. I have 20 programmes to prepare and all to translate before the end of January.*

There were some French Christians living nearby belonging to L'Action Biblique who were extremely kind to Swannie at this time. One day she would be given a large marrow, then a huge pot of marmalade would be left on her doorstep and she was told to help herself to anything in the herb garden whenever she needed it. Swannie was glad of the company of these people and as her French was extremely good she had many lively conversations with them. But often she longed for a friendly voice from home although friends and family did write and she waited impatiently for their letters. Her special friend from Yorkshire, Jenny Wilberforce, was always a great comfort. She sent letters and parcels consistently and Swannie knew that she was never far from her friend's thoughts. During the whole time Swannie was in Morocco, then in Corsica and finally home in England, she was conscious of Jenny's support and she loved her dearly. Many of the incidents reported in this book were provided by Jenny, who painstakingly wrote out pages of Swannie's old letters from Corsica in order to give a better picture of the ten years spent out there.

We can appreciate how much Jenny's support meant to Swannie from the thank-you letter she sent after receiving a parcel for Christmas 1972:

Thank you for the lovely Christmas parcel with the towel and tea inside. The big blanket has not yet arrived but I look forward to it these cold winter nights. I invited the Brandons to drink some of the tea with me and suddenly they asked, "Are you satisfied with what you have done with your life?" Before I knew it I was able to tell them what I had proved down the years, that my hope and confidence lay only in Christ. I know God arranged this time because I never have the opportunity to talk deeply with them. It is so silent here tonight, not a sound but the hum of the refrigerator.

Sometimes Swannie's spirit would get what she called 'ruffled' at times with the pressures that built up. Then she would be unable to prepare the messages for the time they were needed and stress would accumulate as she sat alone in her little room. So it was good when people called and she was able to fix her mind for a short time on something other than the work she was doing. One of her more regular visitors was the local French pastor. She writes in her diary for 16th November 1972:

> *Mons. Pogliano came to lunch today as he has to be in market on Thursdays so comes here for lunch. This makes such a nice change! He considers this his pastoral visit to me as he tries to visit each members of the group once a week. Drees comes on Sunday so I get meat on two days a week now. The doctor has said that Drees has asthma, probably because he shares a room with four men who smoke liberally. He really needs a good wife to look after his creature comforts and pray God will provide someone suitable. In the meantime Mr. Brandon is making an extension at the back. I looked out of the window last night and when I saw what kind of building was going up I immediately thought how good it would be if Drees could live there. It would be a miracle if this did happen but miracles do still happen! His health would improve so much if he had somewhere more decent to live and we would have more time to work in the evenings.*

> *9th January 1973*
> *Jenny's parcel has just come and with it the wonderful oven!*
> *Mr. Brandon fitted it up for me and I shared some of the good things in the parcel with him and his wife. They are so good to me and I shall enjoy the dear little pudding with them when I cook a meal in the oven—I am so thrilled with it. Now I can make the bread that suits me and all kinds of things, including Yorkshire pudding and a roast!*

So there were good times for Swannie despite her isolation. She was thrilled to receive a letter from a G.M.U. colleague saying that the Berber radio programme was now much appreciated in the U.S.A. and many were supporting the work practically. But Swannie was still doing most of the broadcasting in Malaga herself and felt that a real breakthrough would be made if one or two of the Berber Christians felt able to do it. They were understandably reluctant as their voices could quite easily be recognised in Morocco and their families put in danger. There was one Berber professor living in Rabat who was not afraid and offered to broadcast so in 1973 Swannie decided to make a visit to Morocco specifically to meet him and make arrangements. After the visit she wrote in her diary:

> ...Sometimes my heart leaps up with hope, then when I am tired or don't feel well, or Drees doesn't turn up, I despair. But I am learning to keep on an even keel more and am quite sure God is in control and my work is not all in vain. I am now on my way back to Malaga after working for three days with my new contact in Rabat. In Morocco I slept in five different beds so feel rather shattered!

Swannie did not go straight back to Corsica after she had rested a little in Malaga but changed her flight in order to spend a night in Marseilles. This was in order to meet Daisy Marsh, a young English woman who Swannie had heard was preparing radio messages in the Kabyle dialect. She was glad to have the opportunity of meeting this lady and wrote in her diary:

> Daisy Marsh is a woman of about forty and has been born and bred amongst the Kabyles of Algeria. She speaks Kabyl as well as she does English and has done what I suggested and prepared some messages. I heard one and recognised the complete fluency of her language. I feel she should be used at once, so suggested that her messages alternate with mine, one month at a time. I shall still continue on E.L.W.A. weekly.
>
> I don't know yet how the committee (G.M.U.) will receive the suggestion but hope they see it as God requires. The Kabyles should have their chance and Daisy is very good and should be used and encouraged.

125

On returning to Corsica Swannie found that Mr. Brandon had decided to let Drees have the newly built building next to hers. She thought it quite perfect with hot water, electricity and privacy for study. It was to be 15,000 francs a month so Drees had to be consulted in case it was too much to pay but Swannie felt sure a little help from the Berber fund could be obtained as it would make her own work so much easier if he lived near.

At this time Swannie was also working on the translation of some of the Psalms. These were very hard to translate into Shilha and give the correct meaning but she felt strongly that these lovely portions of scripture should not be overlooked and could be of much in benefit to the Berber people. She writes a letter to her friend in England at this time which is a mixture of spiritual and practical comments very typical of Swannie:

I am in desperate need of a good second-hand typewriter so perhaps you could look out for me! Your lovely jar of Marmite came last week—very quickly and thank you! I have heard from Daisy Marsh and she has received a great deal of help to produce her Kabyl programme. She will now come on our programme for four messages and then have her own personal radio programme that I envisage lasting a long time. You will be glad to hear that I had a charming letter from Back to the Bible Broadcasts telling me they have had good reports of my ministry among the Berbers—can't think where this came from! Drees saw his room in the new building and was moved to smile. It has pretty tiles round the sink and in the washroom, a little cupboard and a superb view of the Corsican mountains from the window. Hurry up September when he moves in; he will live like a gentleman with clean sheets and hot and cold water!

The end of 1973 brought Swannie to the close of her fifth year in the Corsican venture. She felt encouraged and much less lonely than she had done twelve months previously but February brought again the onslaught of her terrible rheumatic pains.

She was due to travel to Malaga with Drees two weeks later and he was also having problems. His were not physical like those of Swannie but, as only a very young man, he was suffering even more than she from the isolation of Corsica. He said little but Swannie knew he was desperate for company of his own age and some of the normal relaxations of youth. At times he became morose and when reading over the messages his voice then became lifeless. At this time Swannie was being pressed to engage in the translation of the New Testament and Drees was absolutely essential to this work. To add to the problems a friend of his from Morocco had arrived in Corsica and had a job working in one of the cities for a much higher wage than Drees. The idea of leaving Swannie and the radio work to join his friend in the city was proving a great temptation.

But the crisis seemed to pass and Drees stayed. When they returned from Malaga Swannie began translating again, this time a book called *The Man Jesus*. Together they worked on it every evening until 9.30 or 10 p.m. but Swannie knew it would take many more months of hard work before it was finished. For relaxation Swannie would take out her flute, do some work in the garden or play chess with the set that Jenny had kindly sent out. Drees had promised to stay at least another year which was good but Swannie felt she should return to Morocco in order to find another Berber man who could come out and help her. The future appeared very uncertain to Swannie at times. She wrote:

I have decided to apply for residency and I need two photos.

I also had to have a medical and the lady doctor was quite alarmed at my blood pressure. She ordered me off salt and cheese and told me to rest for fifteen days, but how can I?

Drees needs the extra money the translations are bringing him and we need the literature. Who else can do it if not I? The doctor says I must have a cardiograph and put me on treatment but I am altogether against drugs. The work continues despite all difficulties.

The translation work did take much time, especially when it had to stop periodically for the visits she had to make to Malaga to record. Swannie often wondered what was being achieved during this long 'wilderness' period. She was a person who enjoyed the company of others and social communication. Being alone for a short time didn't worry her but long periods of isolation caused her to doubt the urgency of her work, particularly the very slow task of translation. It was only looking back in later years that she realised how many booklets and Scriptures had been translated into Shilha and the full value of the work done.

Most of the Berber men who had first come out with Swannie to Corsica were by this time either back in Morocco or in jobs that were better paid and enabled them to send more money home to their families. Swannie understood this, realising that their first responsibility was to their families. She never criticised their actions but their absence made her even more grateful for the faithful support of Drees who stayed with her over the most difficult years.

1975 brought a change in circumstances that helped ease the loneliness and frustration for both of them. In early 1974 Drees had returned home for a visit to Morocco and married a beautiful young woman called Fatima. She had not been able to return with him because of passport restrictions but in November 1975 she was finally able to make the journey to Corsica. Swannie's diary shows how she prepared for the young bride's homecoming:

Tomorrow Drees arrives with his little wife. I have just finished arranging their room and have changed Drees's little bed for my big one. It is hard—but they say a bed like this is really best for the body. I have fixed pictures on the walls, all lovely bright flowers I cut out of a calendar and mounted on coloured paper. I've fixed up a pretty flowered curtain and placed a vase of Zinnias on the table with some pretty soap and talcum powder. The studio really sings a welcome to them and I'm glad I got home from Malaga in time to make the room look cosy. But I did leave behind me a large iced cake as the couple were having a little service of blessing there when they arrived from Morocco. I could wait no longer for them as I had a visitor arriving. I have left two pieces of luggage for Drees to bring in the car. I just long to work quietly now in some place I can call home. Once I didn't mind this wandering life but now it seems I can't take it victoriously!

They arrived today and she is very pretty and the opposite of Drees in character as she is extrovert and vivacious. I shall call her Werda, which means 'a rose' in Arabic for she is as lovely as a rose and full of life. She laughs all the time and seems as sharp as a needle. She's never been to school, comes from a poor home, wipes her nose on her hand and tries to push everyone around. I think she is the right one for Drees and I hope that little by little she will learn to be polite and use a handkerchief!

In February 1976 Swannie received the proofs from Malaga of an illustrated booklet she had done called "The Four Spiritual Laws" and was delighted with them. Another book was being translated at the same time and Swannie took the opportunity of asking a G.M.U. colleague who was based at the Malaga Centre to read through the proofs with her. She writes:

May these first pieces of literature be really used by God, for the work has involved years of tears and trials.

November 1976 found Swannie back in Malaga with Drees, his wife and their new baby of four weeks, Yasmine, who was to have a dedication service. The couple then set off for Meknes, presumably for a visit to show the baby to their families, but Swannie felt unsure as to whether they would return to Corsica. She herself tried to settle down typing her third book while spending the Christmas period in Malaga with colleagues and in January returned again to Corsica.

In the summer of 1978 Swannie made another deputation trip to the U.S.A. At the end of it she was thoroughly exhausted and there were important decisions she knew would have to be made. Her home in Corsica was not available until the autumn and colleagues in Malaga were trying to persuade Swannie to move to Malaga permanently and complete her translation work there while continuing with the Berber radio broadcasts. She was tempted, as she could then more easily make periodic trips to Morocco to find and train Berber men to take up the radio work that she knew would soon have to be relinquished. Swannie was by this time nearly seventy and for the first time feeling that perhaps she needed a more comfortable base from which to work.

Was this the time to move permanently to Malaga? she wondered.

Later, in October of that same year, Swannie seemed to have her answer and wrote:

The Word I read encourages me to continue in Corsica while my strength lasts, at least for another year. God can do so much in just a flick of time but I must find somewhere more suitable to live. Transport is my problem—I am in Ajaccio sitting on a seat above the port waiting for the one bus daily to the place where I now live. I have an hour to wait. I don't know why things have to be so hard, probably to teach me patience as I have always been short of that! Drees and Werda did come back and have a nice little house from where he can reach me in ten minutes in the car. A little Corsican couple, Joseph and Mary Grimini have moved into a little cottage down the road and have invited me to stay there. I had a plate of soup with them last night and a lump of dry bread and sheep's milk cheese and they gave me three keys.

One was for the kitchen, one for the big iron gate leading to the second floor outside and the other for the outside toilet. I used them all last night! I have been reading "The Confessions of St. Augustine" and it takes me into another world where Christianity is real. Augustine was a Berber and this thrills me and encourages me to hold on. God surely has a part to play with this race when he selected such a man in the early days of the church. Perhaps there is another such Berber man in Morocco and will respond to my plea for help with the radio programmes before it is too late. I still have eight more chapters to do on the translation of the Gospel of St. John but the days are running out.

Swannie stayed in Corsica until the middle of 1979 and then said goodbye to the country where she had spent ten wilderness years. Berber messages in the Shilha tongue were being broadcast regularly all over Morocco on Trans World Radio and, though much translation had been done there was more to do while living in Malaga. The work for Swannie had not finished—she was just moving over to a different base and God was still the one in control.

Swannie wrote a last letter from Corsica to her dear friend, Jenny:

I still have such a strong sense of some work yet to be done by me. It is the feeling of being held back on a leash, not able to move and yet capable and eager to keep on. The charm is there and I can't break it! I am planning England for July and August then back to Malaga for several months before going into Morocco again to seek out and teach the few young Berber men who have expressed interest in the radio work and willingness to help.

When I was converted I thought I had come to the end of the quest for truth. Now I feel that it is just the beginning, but I see it as the beginning of a new level of understanding much higher than the first. I will not write again from here, dear Jenny, but thank you for all your love and prayers, letters, books and parcels. I could not easily have coped without them.

131

Chapter 14
Still in Business!

SWANNIE WAS ONCE MORE LIVING IN a community—the first time she had done so for many years. This time it was in Malaga, Spain, where some Gospel Missionary Union missionaries had based after all Christian workers had been expelled from Morocco. When taken over by G.M.U. in 1968, El Atabal was an area in Malaga consisting of just a few small buildings; but it was considered suitable ground for expansion of the Arabic radio station that was hoped would grow over the years. At the expulsion of the missionaries they had been granted the right to apply for entrance into Morocco but only on visitors' visas that enabled them to stay for just three months at a time. Many took advantage of this and made regular trips to Morocco, taking literature and encouraging the national believers who made up a large percentage of the growing 'underground' church. The ladies working in the orphanages and others in secular employment had been allowed to stay and they too remained working members of the church.

Swannie's work did not greatly change while in Malaga. Her time was still mostly spent in the radio ministry and literature for the Berbers of the Middle Atlas. She was anxious to make the regular visits to Morocco allowed after she had settled down in El Atabal which, by the time she arrived in the autumn of 1979, was expanding into an estate consisting of rooms for printing and broadcasting as well as homes suitable for the growing community of workers. The only difference was that Swannie was now one of many and at first it was difficult for her to adjust to that situation. It must have been quite as difficult for her colleagues as well for Swannie was used to doing things in her own time and was the first to admit that everything connected with Berber work was first priority in her mind. She was soon to realise that her colleagues also had priorities and were equally involved in outreach to Morocco and other Arab states! Both the printing press and radio station were still in the stage of development and often the workload was extremely heavy for those manning the equipment.

Swannie tried to understand how busy the centre was becoming but often grew impatient because of her crowded workload. She had been broadcasting Berber messages for ten years by that time and was anxious to keep these going, but she was also busy producing booklets in Shilha for the Scripture Gift Mission. She had also an extended ministry that had not been anticipated while Drees was working with her in Corsica. This was the training of three Berber men for the actual broadcasting of the Berber programmes in the dialect of the central region of Morocco. Swannie writes:

I was able to make a short visit to Morocco that brought about a new development I had not foreseen and which means that I shall be staying here in El Atabal longer than I thought. 'Retirement' has never been a favourite word of mine and I shall never lay down my responsibilities to the Berbers wherever I live, but I have been directed to help in the relinquishing of the radio programme into Berber hands. I am part of the centre at Malaga now and Corsica is receding into the background of my consciousness. I am becoming involved with the life here and what happens to the team as a whole affects me and the work I do. I must admit it is a continual grief to me that as yet I have had to work alone as far as the Berber language is concerned but am grateful for all the help given to me in other directions. That the radio talks could be taken over by native Berbers seems to me an ideal solution.

Maynard Yoder was a G.M.U. colleague in charge of administration at El Atabal at this time and he was only too aware of the situation. He suggested that Swannie make another short visit to Morocco, this time with his wife, Margaret, and himself. Swannie was only too delighted to do this, as can be seen from the following extracts in her diary:

Morocco, 13 October 1979

It is wonderful to be here again. I am in Fes and last evening helped a Sous Berber who has lived in this area for many years to read some of our literature. He was soon reading slowly but surely but for the sake of recording at the right speed to test his voice I dictated and he wrote it down and read it again in his own familiar tongue. He is going to practice so that he can read my scripts.

This morning we go to Ain-Leuh and Azrou and tomorrow I shall be recording with another Berber who can read the script more fluently.

His name is Hafadowi and he is not a Sous Berber but belongs to the central Berber area, Zain. There is always a difference in vocabulary with the various tribes but usually the words can be understood. There is another exciting development! Neither Arabic nor French letters really belong to the Berber tongue and I have been told that four men in high positions in government, themselves Berbers, are pushing for a resurrection of the original language, to be written as well as spoken. There have been lessons in the newspapers and I will work on one of these while in Meknes. The Zaian Berber and I are going to write to each other in this script—there are about forty symbols and the words are read from left to right.

15 October
This morning I worked with Hafadawi and have left him some books to study. I will come back soon to work with him on programmes that I hope will be on the air by next Easter. There will be many disappointments but we are nearer the goal than ever before. Maynard will bring the equipment for recording at that time.

On her return to Malaga in November, Swannie decided to get down to learning the new Berber script. The house that had been allotted to her in El Atabal was sufficient for her needs but badly in need of some renovation. Soon she was suffering from the bronchitis that always plagued her and was exacerbated by damp conditions. It was with some relief that a team of six workmen arrived in December to work on her home. They put in a washbowl next to the toilet, hot water and a mosquito door. Most important of all to Swannie, they cut out the top panel of the front door and put in a window so that air could be allowed in and she could breathe freely.

In January 1980 Swannie was surprised to hear that she was to go to Morocco again, this time by air, in order to meet the three men she felt would be suitable for broadcasting. She flew to Tangier and then made her way to Fes in order to work with Felaki, who was only free to work with her in the evenings. From there she went to Meknes to work again with Hafadowi and lastly she was able to meet Hemsa who lived. In Fes.

This was again only a short visit and the work of two months had to be packed into two days; but Swannie returned to Malaga quite encouraged. In spite of the makeshift quarters and the lack of heating at the places she stayed something had been accomplished. The spirit of the men was good and they were all eager to give as much time as they could to learning the techniques of broadcasting. But Swannie definitely needed to spend longer periods of time with them and for that a suitable place must be found where she could base. It was decided that Rabat was the best place for this as she could travel by bus to the other towns and visit the men on their home ground.

At the end of January Swannie was back in her renovated home in El Atabal and thanking God for the comfort of it! She had to admit to her distress that the nomadic life no longer suited her and she longed for the comfort of El Atabal while she was in Morocco in a way that she definitely did not think was spiritual!

Old age was not bringing with it the tranquillity Swannie had hoped. In fact she was much more conscious of how irritable she could sometimes become than her colleagues ever guessed. She prayed that she would be kept sweet and not become unduly upset by provocation and difficulties. Swannie was very aware of her own shortcomings and acknowledged that although her mind was sharp and she was grateful for that, her tongue could sometimes be almost as sharp! She had been asking God for patience and courage for years, thinking she lacked in both those area, and there is evidence to show that her prayers were answered. Swannie was a woman of principle and sometimes her high standards were almost too difficult for herself to attain, much less her colleagues and friends. But underneath the sever and ordered exterior was a warm and sympathetic heart. Swannie was always there to listen and help those in need.

On the 13th March it was Swannie's 70th birthday and, perhaps for that reason, found herself thinking about home and her friends in England when she rose that morning. However, she spent the day working as usual and then made her way to the home of one of her colleagues in El Atabal.

She had been invited to a cold supper there before the weekly prayer meeting but Swannie had no idea that anyone knew it was her birthday. To her surprise as she entered the door she found the living room full of people and a table spread with delicious sandwiches and salads. The secret had been wonderfully kept and Swannie found herself enjoying a marvellous surprise party with all her friends. She was given a beautiful kettle so that she could easily boil the water for her own special brand of English tea. Swannie was very touched but made the wry comment that '…now I have my own little kettle perhaps I can conclude that my own little home in which to hold the tea parties will follow!'

Before too long Swannie received a letter from Hemsa in the ancient Berber script saying that he had received the lessons, so on her next trip to Morocco she visited him first in Rabat. There was only had a makeshift bed and a table in the tiny room provided there, but it was enough for Swannie to stay a few days and discuss the coming radio presentation with him.

Swannie then went on to Meknes and stayed at Derb Skat. Hafadowi had a small shop selling school books and newspapers and as he was not married and had few family commitments, he came round to see Swannie whenever possible. But the business had to have his constant attention and often it was only after closing time that he could be free. But he was progressing even better than the others. His zeal was contagious and Swannie was much encouraged as she worked with Hafadowi and thought it quite possible that in time he could take over the Berber broadcasts.

At this time Swannie was also brought in touch with another young man, a Berber Christian called El Kabir who also lived in Rabat. He was able to visit Swannie daily and she found him a great help in translation and correct pronunciation.

The search for a suitable place for Swannie to stay during her three-monthly visits to Morocco did not materialise until she returned at the end of September. By this time the urgency of the situation had been mentioned to Gordon McRostie and his wife, Daphne, who were G.M.U. missionaries living in Rabat at that time with his family. They took Swannie round to different agencies but there was not much choice, the only apartment that seemed at all suitable being in the Arab quarters near the town centre. But as it was on the first floor of a block and looked moderately clean, with a bedroom, living room, small kitchen and bathroom, Swannie decided to take it.

All through 1980 Swannie travelled backwards and forwards from Malaga to Morocco. When she arrived in Rabat she would make herself as comfortable as possible, rest a little while and then work with the men there before going on to Fes and Meknes. She was making progress particularly with Hafadowi so she decided to go from Rabat visit every two weeks and visit him. The journey by bus wearying, but each time they met Swannie felt exhilarated by Hafadowi's obvious enthusiasm. He could not wait to do the recording and was thrilled to hear his own voice giving out the gospel message in the Berber tongue.

Back in her flat in Rabat, Swannie still spent much time on her own alone so was thrilled when three of the older Berber girls from the orphanages started to visit her. Two were from Ain Leuh and one from Azrou and very often two of the young men would turn up as well. The most regular of these was Jamal, a young Berber who wanted to go as a student to Capenwray Bible School in England, and Swannie was helping him with his application for this. Another was Hamid who had a job at the Azrou orphanage and would arrive whenever he was not working. Swannie was particularly fond of Hamid. He was the son of Si Mohammed, a good friend of hers from early days in Demnate, and often as a young boy he had been her guide as she visited Berbers living in the Middle Atlas Mountains. The young people all seemed thrilled to visit Swannie. She would make a meal and they would spend the evening chatting happily together over different events and problems. The company of these young people greatly cheered Swannie while she worked in the Arab quarters of Rabat.

Swannie's old friends at the Ain Leah Orphanage, Ellen and Emergene, were still there but finding it increasingly difficult with the passing years and the increase in the number of children. They were older than Swannie and were often weary as there was often a lack of permanent help at the orphanage. Whenever she had the opportunity Swannie would go out by bus to try and assist in the many jobs entailed in the running of the home and the care of the children.

Swannie enjoyed her visits to Morocco, although on her return she was exhausted and each time it was taking longer to recuperate from all the travelling she was doing in Morocco. She was expecting more of herself than physical limitations would allow but perhaps because of this the responsibility of training the Berber men seemed even more important to Swannie. She was conscious of the fact that she would only be able to continue the radio work in Malaga for a year or two longer.

In February 1981 Swannie was again in Rabat but not feeling very well. The cold weather, dismal atmosphere in the small apartment and the continual travelling and then sitting down for hours to write, did not help. She had an infection and her throat and ears were unbearably painful. Suddenly she seemed to be living in a kind of nightmare and felt sure that she must leave the apartment in Rabat at once or have a complete breakdown and the radio work would then collapse.

If she had been in good health Swannie would have laughed at the thoughts surging through her mind at this time. Her usual sense of comedy would have come to the fore and grasped the ludicrous situation. A woman of seventy years old single-handedly holding up such an important work! In fact she might well have drawn one of her famous 'sketches' of a frail old woman with the Berber radio floating dimly away in the distance. But she was more sick than she realised and in her depression Swannie felt that the endeavours of her whole life had come to nothing. She was at her lowest ebb.

But help was at hand for when Daphne and Gordon heard about Swannie's condition, they immediately took her into their home, demanding that she stay until she was fully recovered. They knew how debilitating the winter could be in Rabat and how quickly the spirit could get depressed. A visit from the doctor and a few weeks of warmth and relaxation among friends would make all the difference.

And it did! But when Swannie was feeling better and they took her back to the little apartment there was another shock in store. She opened the door and water seeped around her feet and an awful smell emanated from it. This was the last straw. Colleagues decided that the damp, depressing apartment in Rabat was no longer a fit place for Swannie to live in. When she needed to stay in Morocco it must be with her colleagues at Ain Leuh or Meknes and Swannie had to agree. She writes in her diary for April:

I go now to Ain Leuh and thank God it is not Rabat but a place familiar to me and the scene of my nomadic days. I hope to finish the gospel translation there and also arrange with Jemal the details of his stay in England at Capenwray. El-Kebir and Hafadowi are still working on messages and it is thrilling to hear Falaki's voice now on the air. He is speaking for six weeks and is the one who is being troubled by police interrogation. The messages are those recorded last year after I came into Morocco to train the men. I am preparing some more now because they have had no bible study training and cannot yet compose their own messages. I think soon there will be some who can do this as well as record. After the six weeks Hafadowi will be on the air and then maybe El-Kabir. The poor, friendly Berbers keep my loneliness at bay and I feel as though things are moving at last. Drees was faithful for so many years and I trust he and Werda will have a lovely life together. They visited me in Malaga on their return to Corsica where Drees has obtained a better job. My heart is with them but now they are no longer with me and I must give these last years to training the other young men willing to take over the Berber radio work.

Chapter 15
Farewell to the 'Mission Field'

IN THE SUMMER OF 1981 SWANNIE had made a last trip up the Middle Atlas. If she went again to Morocco she felt that probably she would never experience the wild beauty of the mountains in the same way, belonging to her beloved Berbers. Perhaps the best way to portray Swannie's feelings at this time is in a letter sent to her friend, Jenny, during that time:

I am sat here where I little expected to be again—in the heart of Berber land and among my old semi-nomadic friends of the Middle Atlas. If I lift my eyes from the table where I write I can see the bare escarpment of Ighud beyond the near fields of barley where the Berbers are harvesting now. Their resonant chatter and laughter, interspersed with bursts of singing, do not interfere with my thoughts any more than the bird songs, which are quite non-stop in the cherry trees below me.

Ahead of me beyond a field where sheep graze and more cherry orchards make patchwork with fields of ripening wheat, rise up the old familiar twin slopes of Tishiniuwin looking exactly like two pyramids.

Behind me lies the little village of Tufstel nestling at the foot of the lower slopes of Dada-Hamu with thick forests running for hundreds of miles along the slopes of the Middle Atlas.

I journeyed through them last week to the source of one of Morocco's rivers, the Com Arabia, and how I wished my friends back in England could have been with me to see the awesome grandeur of hill and valley, forest and lake. A group of Berbers gathered round me as I left the van in which I was travelling and I sat with them for an hour or so listening and trying out the dialect I am familiar with against their somewhat different vocabulary. The same old warm friendliness I had met in the days when I shared their life more closely with them was still there. I was grateful for this because to reach the source of the river I had to cross a swiftly flowing stream and was firmly seized and saved from slipping on the wet surface, as I had done years ago.

We caught a glimpse of the apes that inhabit the forest. I remembered their casual attitude from the days when I used to go through their territory early in the morning with my old friend, Aberbash, both of us walking and my belongings on the back of a donkey.

I was urgently pressed by one Berber family to go again to one of the tents by the lake of Afen-Ourir where I camped with them before. I did sit with them for a while but hadn't the courage to spend the night there. It seems I have grown more fussy and less accommodating over the years but I enjoyed the time I spent again with this little family. Years ago I was at their wedding and it was the man's father, Assou, who welcomed me before. He died about the same time as my friend Aberbash.

I have moved into the habit of old folk and am reminiscing.

But I do not apologise for this as I like to remind myself of the days before I had to leave my special Berber friends for a ministry more far-reaching for them but less enjoyable to me.

I am here of course because I had to leave Rabat and stay at Ain Leuh. It is in a beautiful part of Morocco and I often think that when I die I should like my ashes to be sprinkled somewhere in the mountain forests. I look many times upon the loveliness here and thank God for the faulty plumbing that soaked my apartment and drove me out of the Rabat area altogether. There are some flies in the ointment here—but where in life is there anywhere free of 'flies'?

While at the orphanage I have continued my work of radio and literature. The men visit me regularly here now instead of me having to make the tiring journeys by bus to reach them. Despite time lost the goal is now in sight. Our technician is coming from Spain and we plan to record the prepared messages in Rabat before I leave Morocco. I have also finished writing the Gospel of John in the original script of Tifinagh and Hafadowi and I are in the process of re-checking it.

Although I leave Morocco now and I suppose some folk might say I am retiring, this is not exactly correct. For at least six months I shall be engaged in preparing the script for printing. Since, because of lack of necessary facilities this must be done by hand, it will be a laborious business. But I hope to be in my own little home somewhere in England to finish it. There I will have no distractions and trust it will be finished before I again visit our print shop in Malaga for its actual production.

I hope to visit the U.S.A. and Canada to make my final farewells to all those over there who have prayerfully and practically shared the work with me.

The visit to the U.S.A. that Swannie had planned for later that year did not materialise. This was probably due to fatigue after the stress of the recordings by the two Berber men and the severe concentration that this entailed. She writes:

...all this and then the strain of getting the recordings through customs under the present tense atmosphere as well as the cleaning up and packing at Ain Leuh has taken its toll. I'm whacked! My head aches and I long to get among friends and rest.

Arrangements had been made by colleagues in Malaga to help Swannie with arrangements for travelling home and last-minute packing jobs, etc., and in her last letter from 'the mission field' to Jenny she writes:

The Operation Mobilisation van is bringing a worker here from Belgium and Gordon (McRostie) says that his brother will arrange for my goods to be taken back to their centre in Bromley. Please pray that all my stuff will get through soon as it consists of my winter clothing, blankets, etc., and especially the books I need to continue my work on the Tifinagh gospel. I hate the thought of again travelling around but am hoping to make a trip to the U.S.A. next year as I have not yet bid them farewell and must encourage the people there to continue supporting the work amongst the Berbers.

I am really writing this letter to send you my special thanks and love for all the years you have given me a friendship that few can ever boast of having. My work has been truly your work and I have been conscious of your rock-like support in all the heavy seas I have travelled through. You have more than made up for any lack of fellowship I might have suffered at times in my work.

Dearly would I love my own little place and put an end to the loneliness I now feel as I leave El Atabal.

In October 1981, Swannie received the last of her luggage from Belgium, for which she was very grateful as the winter chills of England were already becoming a problem. But it was to be some time before she was settled into the little home of her own she wanted so much. When it arrived at last it was in Devon, the county where Swannie had been born and which she loved. Her last years must deserve a chapter or two of their own.

Chapter 16
Home in England

SINCE HER RETURN TO ENGLAND FROM Malaga in 1981 Swannie had lived in many different places. Some of these had been provided by kind friends and for which she was very grateful, others she rented because they were available at the time and suited her needs. Not one of them did Swannie think of as a permanent home.

'Somewhere,' she would say to friends, 'there must be a little place for me that I shall know immediately it is to be my last home on earth!'

It was November 1984 before Swannie was finally in the small cottage in the market town of Kingsbridge, South Devon, which proved to be that home.

Some years before Swannie had been working with the G.M.U. team in Malaga when a young woman came out from England to help in the print shop. Her name was Angela Smith and as they got to know each other better she and Swannie became good friends. They kept in touch and after returning to England, Angela invited her to take a holiday in Kingsbridge where her parents had a guesthouse. Swannie was glad of the opportunity of doing this and found Alan and Rose Smith to be extremely kind. Their hospitality at Ashleigh House did much to make Swannie's holiday a time to remember and she didn't want to leave. In fact, she was falling in love with the whole area and began wondering if this might be the place where God intended her to settle and work while still carrying on with her commitment to the Berbers.

Indeed it was a very congenial area and much warmer than a lot of places in England; a factor with Swannie as she hoped this might help control the bronchitis that had plagued her since youth. The surrounding countryside was considered some of the most beautiful in England, with Dartmoor only a drive away and a tidal estuary running through the small town making it picturesque and very appealing to someone like Swannie with such an artistic temperament. Already she could imagine herself taking bracing walks along the wooded lanes and sitting beside the estuary. There were also several places of worship in Kingsbridge and she had very much enjoyed the services at the Baptist church that she attended with Alan and Rose.

'I could really settle here,' she confessed to the couple, 'something about it feels right for me!'

Swannie had always been one to trust her instincts but listened to Alan as he cautioned her about making any decisions too quickly. He had seen too many holidaymakers take a strong liking to the area and make a move they later regretted.

'Living here is different altogether than spending a few weeks in the middle of summer,' he reasoned. 'Kingsbridge can be very quiet and even dull to some people in the winter.'

Swannie knew all about living in isolated places and quietness had never worried her so what her friends said did not put her off at all but she took their advice and started to give the matter a lot of prayer and thought. Later, when it became known that a small cottage was coming up for sale Swannie could not help feeling that it was God's direction and asked to be allowed to view it. When she heard that the address was Baptist Lane she was excited and even more convinced.

The cottage was small but very 'olde world' and Swannie was thrilled with it. She was also delighted to find that it was almost opposite the Baptist church as the address had suggested and that was part of her specifications for a new home. Had she not always wanted a little place of her own that was so near a church that she could worship independently without travelling worries? The cottage was perfectly situated for that and had the added bonus of being only a few minutes from the shopping area that was on the main street. To Swannie the way was perfectly clear; the little cottage in Kingsbridge, Devon, was the answer to her prayers.

So negotiations started and in November of the same year everything was ready for Swannie to move in. The cottage had been already fairly modernised but was in need of fresh paintwork and repairs, also a few alterations to make it more suitable for Swannie's personal needs. She was thrilled with it all and wrote:

I am now in my new home, a delightful little cottage in Kingsbridge, a market town in South Devon. I have come full circle now, as I was born in a cottage not far north from here, also in Devon. My roots were not in Eastbourne, though I surely had to be taken there for a time by the one who directed my steps as surely then as he has done now. Most of all I have been blessed with new friends here. Alan and Rose could not have been more helpful; in fact, I don't know how I would have managed the move without them. When their daughter Angela came to Malaga and later designed the cover for the initial tract I wrote in the original Berber language, I little thought her family would be instrumental in directing me to my future home. They have welcomed me into the area with a fullness of love and that makes me feel I belong

148

here already. Alan and a friend came in his van and removed all my belongings to Kingsbridge. He and Rose have done wonders to beautify this cottage and give me the comfort I am now enjoying day and night. I hope the friends who have followed my somewhat kaleidoscopic life in the past will now feel free to visit this dear little place and we can have a cosy Devon tea together!

By Christmas Swannie was comfortably settled in and enjoying a place that was completely her own. She had not had the satisfaction of living in a home that was really her own since the little nuella that was built for her in Morocco, and she revelled in it. She could eat when she wanted, sleep when she was tired and, very important to Swannie, entertain who she wanted!

Swannie had many plans for entertaining and showed great hospitality to both neighbours and friends. Peter and Sue were the couple living next door and they were soon on friendly terms as Peter immediately offered to help carry the furniture indoors when Alan's van arrived. They had a family and often the boys would come in to sit with Swannie and listen to the wonderful tales she had to tell about her life abroad.

But the Berber friends she had left behind in Morocco were still ever-present in Swannie's heart and mind. The men carrying on so faithfully the work she had started needed practical support as well as prayer. Swannie knew that often these men were in grave danger and her task now was to tell others about them and the work they were doing. She must also keep in touch despite the thousands of miles that separated them; Swannie's earnest desire was that she would keep well enough to visit Morocco and see them all again before too long. She was given the health and strength to do this and in 1986 Swannie visited Hafadowi in order to complete the translation of John's Gospel into the original Berber language, which they had worked on together for so long.

Hafadowi was planning to marry a young Berber girl named

Muna, but in 1988 he suffered a bad car accident and Swannie felt she must go out to Morocco to see how her good friend was progressing and also to meet his new wife. Arriving in Meknes just after the couple had returned from their wedding, Swannie was thrilled to be able to sit down with them and talk. Hafadowi was recovering well from the accident and the couple were obviously very happy together so all was well except for the fact that their living accommodation was far from satisfactory. The couple had just a one-roomed apartment which they shared with Hafadowi's mother who, though she had sleeping arrangements elsewhere, had to share everything else with them. Swannie knew just how hard Hafadowi worked on the radio talks and translation work, never failing her whatever the personal cost, and she felt his need keenly. His own little business had at times been neglected and he now had a wife to support as well as the mother he had always provided for. Hafadowi had also become a leader in the local underground church and Swannie felt that he might be the one to establish the Christian work in Morocco once more. She resolved to do all she could to raise more support for him and his family when she returned home.

As well as going to Morocco, Swannie was that year given the privilege of attending a conference in Priego, Spain, with around twenty young couples whom she had found out were engaged in Berber evangelism. Throughout her ten years in Corsica, Swannie had hoped and prayed for others to join her, particularly those deeply committed enough to learn the Berber language and live amongst them. It was a real encouragement for Swannie to meet with those young people and see at last what she felt to be an answer to her prayers.

To Swannie's surprise the next year she was asked if she would like to be one of a party from Plymouth who were going on a trip to Israel.

This was a country she had always longed to visit and though Swannie was thrilled at the thought, she was troubled by the thought of her health, which had been bad over the summer months. She had suffered from acute pain in one of her legs that had become so unbearable she had been admitted into hospital. It had eased a little by that time so she was definitely giving the Israel trip some thought and the fact that her good friend, Audrey Clarke, a capable nurse who ran a care home in a small village near Kingsbridge, was planning to go did much to help Swannie decide.

So October 1989 Swannie was on the plane again, this time to visit Israel, a place she had never visited but had read much about. It turned out to be a wonderful trip and Swannie was amazed at how far she was able to walk. They travelled first to Jerusalem and then north to Galilee and Swannie recalls in her diary:

> *There is a verse in the Bible that reads 'When I am weak then I am strong' and I think this strength must have been given to me. I have walked miles and miles and climbed quite a hundred stone steps!*
>
> *Our guide is very good but really draining us all with the itinerary but I am determined to miss nothing. The Garden Tomb was exactly as I had imagined from the Bible description and Gethsemane was strangely quiet with such gnarled old olive trees. It might have been one of these that Christ knelt under the last night before he was crucified. Tomorrow we move north to Galilee.*

Despite her health problems in the summer, Swannie had much reason to rejoice that same year when at last the translation of John's Gospel that she and Hafadowi had worked on for so long was published. In December 1989 she wrote a prayer letter to friends, very much in her own colourful style:

151

...now I can give you the last report you will receive from me because I have at last seen the completion of a work that seemed at times to be never reaching fulfilment and which taxed my faith and perseverance to the utmost. I passed through many tunnels of dark disquiet, over ridges of weary climbing, and across turbulent waters that seemed uncrossable before reaching the firm ground and wide horizons that faith in provides. John's Gospel in the Berber language, printed in the original alphabet (supposedly preceding the Greek, and quite similar to it, by six hundred years) is now finished. It is quite a handsome production in a cover of royal blue and gold. It holds also the same Gospel in Arabic to help those who are just learning the ancient script. Wycliffe Translators must be thanked and are truly appreciated for all the expertise they have given to this work since my official retirement in 1981 when I had to return to England with the translation only in its first stages. I would like to pay tribute to the support and encouragement given me by Brian Bull and his wife in spite of their other commitments in relation to their busy schedule directing the language side of Mission in the Mediterranean area.

Swannie's main translation work was now complete but still her mind was in Morocco and she particularly worried about her Berber colleague and his young wife, Muna. She had made many friends in and around the Kingsbridge area and took every possible opportunity to speak to them about her past life in Corsica and her Berber friends still working in Morocco. Often she would visit local churches and other places to show the slides she had been able to accumulate over the years. Much interest was shown and practical support given but as the years passed Swannie's longing to visit again the country she called her second home only deepened. She knew that any further visit she was able to make to Morocco would be her last, and certainly a bonus!

In 1990 she received a call from Gordon McRostie and his wife who was then working with the Arab church in Brussels.

He was able to provide up-to-date news from Morocco and also sent greetings from Hafadowi saying Muna had recently given birth to a baby girl they had named Rifka. Though Swannie longed to go and see them her health was now preventing her. In 1990 she had suffered from a weakness in the right lung and spent some time again in hospital. Then she had gone to the care home in Strete to convalesce and those weeks had helped boost her strength. But Swannie knew now that she would never again be able to travel overseas on her own. So she put another visit to Morocco completely out of her mind and life went on as usual with its steady round of responsibilities and activities. She had many friends in Kingsbridge and it would be impossible to mention them all but she never stopped appreciating their loving concern for her as she grew older and more dependent on others.

It was 1993 and Swannie had passed her eighty-third birthday when the last big surprise came. She was then attending the Evangelical Church in Kingsbridge and had become a good friend of Tim Gocher, who played the organ there and was a talented musician. He often called round to see Swannie and they had good discussions together and as they talked he could not help but notice the faraway look in Swannie's eyes as she talked of her years in Morocco and her dear Berber friends who she was getting more and more convinced she would never see again. One day he asked if she felt well enough to travel to Morocco if the opportunity arose and Swannie waited a moment before replying. She was only too conscious of the weakness of her body and the frailty that was descending on her with age and admitted so to Tim, adding sadly that it would never again be possible to travel alone as she had done so often in the past. Then she tossed her head in typical Swannie defiance and told him that it was not her health that was the worry—she could pray about that—it was her age that was the problem!

When Tim said in his usual quiet and humble way that he

would like to accompany her to Morocco if she would let him, Swannie could not believe what she was hearing. A companion to help share the burden of travelling and take away the fear and loneliness of the long flight? Someone to enjoy with her the beauties of Morocco and to whom she could introduce all her old friends? The prospect was overwhelming to Swannie who had travelled so often on her own and had often longed for someone to share it all with. But of course it could not be…it was too much to ask of anyone especially a young man like Tim. After all, she was an old lady and would no doubt need a lot more help than even she herself could imagine.

Tim remained adamant. If Swannie felt able to physically make the journey then he would very much appreciate the opportunity of accompanying her to Morocco. It was a pleasure because he would get to see the country that her stories and descriptions had made him long to visit—and she would have someone to see to arrangements and make sure she didn't overdo things.

So Swannie made her final trip to Morocco in September 1993 and what a memorable time for both of them. They travelled from place to place in Morocco visiting friends Swannie had known in years gone by and introducing them to Tim. Together they tracked down one old man Swannie had not seen for nearly thirty years and they greeted each other with obvious delight. They were able to visit Hafadowi and Muna, settled now with their little girl into an apartment much more suitable for their needs and the work he was doing, much to the relief of Swannie. Everything was fresh and new to Tim and his eyes gloried in the scenery with its hills and valleys, deserts and forests. Swannie made him known to everyone she knew and was delighted at how well he fitted in with her friends and their totally different way of life. It was wonderful for her to show him Derb Skat, the ex-palace of a princess so often talked about and, Tim said, looking almost exactly as Swannie had described it. This was a place of many memories for Swannie as it had been her home for several years and her spiritual base for even longer.

After Meknes they went on to Azrou and spent a couple of nights in the orphanage at Ain Leuh with the two elderly missionaries and the many children they still looked after despite their age.

Then it was Khemisset, Rabat and finally Casablanca where they boarded the plane for home. Exhausted they looked across at each other and smiled. What a wonderful trip it had been! Swannie beamed at Tim as the engine revved up and the huge plane cruised along the runway and then soared high into the sky. Where were the nerves she had always suffered from when flying? Someone next to her who she knew and trusted made all the difference. Swannie sat back and relaxed, thanking God once again for sending Tim when she needed so badly to make one last precious visit to Morocco. Tim sat back and thanked God for bringing them safely back to England after all the traumatic experiences he had shared with Swannie!

chapter 17
Waiting Time Again

THE NEXT FEW YEARS OFTEN DID seem like 'waiting time' for Swannie. In fact, she often commented wryly that most of her life had been spent waiting and she hoped the results were worth waiting for! She had faith in the verse from the Bible that reads: 'There is a time and a season for everything.' (Ecc.1.3)

Her years in Kingsbridge had provided Swannie with many friends and she was very distressed when one of these, Alan Smith, passed away on 3rd October, 1995, after having a massive heart attack. He and his wife Rose had been the means of Swannie finding her home in Kingsbridge and introducing her to life there. They were always there when she needed a helping hand and she was to miss sorely Alan's frequent visits to have a chat or help with odd jobs around the house.

Later her Berber friend, Hafadowi, a trusted colleague in the radio work, became ill. He was only a young man but had never fully recovered from a motor accident in earlier years but he had seemed healthy and happy with his wife and little daughter when Swannie saw him last in 1993. They had a new home, much more roomy and convenient for the work he was doing and Hafadowi was his usual smiling and charming self. But in 1997 his kidneys were failing and despite all the medical attention he was receiving and help given by G.M.U. colleagues, the illness proved fatal and he died on 28th September of that same year.

Swannie could hardly believe it and grieved sorely for the loss of her good friend and co-worker. She grieved also for the young wife and little daughter left behind. She had been in constant touch with the family during the whole period of Hafadowi's illness but had felt convinced that God would heal him. As well as a beloved friend, was he not the one man entrusted with the burden of the radio work that she had started herself in 1969? All Swannie's hopes had been centred on a man she thought would enable the radio work to flourish and become more widespread among his own Berber people.

God had other plans, however, and throughout the times of grief Swannie was being taught the lesson of acceptance. The Berber radio work would continue, and is still doing so to this day, because it never had been dependent upon any one man or woman…only God held the reins.

Swannie was realising that even now in her late seventies there were lessons she still had to learn, and often the hard way. But how she missed her two loyal friends. One had been a quiet, considerate Englishman who lived so near and was always ready to chat and give comfort as well as practical advice; the other a big, strong Berber with a bright smile and so much energetic zeal that, even though he lived thousands of miles away from Swannie, had been such an important part of her life and the continuation of the Berber work she loved so dearly.

Swannie found it very hard to understand why a young man like Hafadowi had been taken in the prime of his life. How much harder it would be for his young wife, who had been a

157

Christian for so few years, to try and understand. She tried to find words to comfort the young widow when she spoke to her on the telephone but to Swannie's surprise found that she was being comforted and helped by Muna's simple trust in God and her thankfulness for the years she had been able to share with Hafadowi. Swannie's faith was renewed as she listened and she began to appreciate afresh the truth of God's sovereignty. Nothing ever took him by surprise!

It had always been the hope and prayers of the G.M.U. missionaries in Morocco that the church should eventually be in the hands of national believers. This had become increasingly possible since the last missionary workers were evacuated in 1969. Swannie had been one of the last to leave and, as we read earlier, had made many trips back and forth to Morocco. She was very fearful at times for the safety of her friends in the church there and wrote regularly to some of them in order to be up-to-date with events.

This time of waiting was also proving a time of great prayer for Swannie. She was realising that though her point of contact in the work had changed, she was very much in the front line. Now her task was to pray for Morocco in a way that she had never been able to do in her earlier and busier days. She was also now in a better position to inform others about the underground church in Morocco and those Christians meeting together so faithfully, and get their support.

Swannie showed her slides regularly to different audiences and always tried to make these times 'an occasion.' Even though she was getting too old for much formal entertaining, her door was always open for coffee and a chat, and sometimes mint tea if the visitor was used to the customs of Morocco. In England the tradition was to have sandwiches and tea after a slide show but on Saturday, 28th February, 1998, Swannie really excelled herself. It had been arranged that she give a talk and show slides to a small group at the Evangelical Church in Kingsbridge. Unknown to most of them, she ordered delicious pizzas to be delivered from Polly's Pizzas at exactly nine o'clock when she would have finished her talk. The small market town had only recently acquired its fast-food delivery service but Swannie was ready to take advantage of it. How the audience enjoyed their unexpected supper and what an illustration of Swannie's initiative. She still liked to keep up with the times even at the age of eighty-eight!

But this surge of energy did not last. Swannie's health had been deteriorating badly since 1997 and only three nights after the enjoyable talk at the church she was taken into Derriford Hospital in Plymouth. Whilst there she suffered a severe stroke which resulted in complete paralysis down the right side of her body.

After being discharged from hospital Swannie had to say farewell to the little cottage in Kingsbridge where she had lived so happily for nearly fifteen years. She went to live in Strete Lodge, a care home owned by her friend Audrey that Swannie had visited very often in the past and where she felt quite comfortable. But because of the severity of her condition it was impossible for Swannie to stay there permanently and later in the year she was moved to a nursing home in the area where she could be given more medical attention.

At times Swannie felt low with the constrictions her body imposed and she longed for the independence she once had. But her spirit remained strong, as did her sense of humour if we can go by one scribbled entry of hers that reads: '...I have shingles down the left arm now and am growing more like Job each day!'

Although her right arm was paralysed, Swannie tried hard to write with her left hand and often the result was not just as legible as she would have liked. Eve and Tom Gilkes, members of her church who visited Swannie regularly, helped her in this writing project. She also found them invaluable in many other ways during her time in the nursing home. Tom would help sort out her business and financial worries and Eve was there encouraging and supporting in any practical way she could. When Swannie's left-hand writing became too scribbled to read clearly, Eve suggested asking visitors to write down a few comments. This they were glad to do and so there are short written accounts of Swannie's daily life in the nursing home until the end of 1998. Swannie also kept scribbling notes and making up little poems, often satirical, until almost the end of her life.

There were many other visitors during 1998 and their presence always brought comfort to Swannie, who only had one sister left of her own immediate family. This sister, Pat, visited whenever she could but her home was many miles away and she too was getting older. A good friend, Jenny, who had supported Swannie so faithfully over the years lived a long way away in Yorkshire and was only able to visit occasionally. But when Swannie was able to have a phone installed they were both often in touch with her.

Swannie particularly appreciated the visits of Pete and Sue Hammet, a young couple who had lived in the cottage next door to her for some years. They had three boys and Swannie was very fond of them all. Pete had a great respect for Swannie and during the last months of her life he visited almost every day. She also appreciated the helpful visits of Tom and Eve who saw to so many of the problems that would otherwise have been a great worry. Perhaps no one will ever know how much the visits of all Swannie's friends meant to her and how they helped cheer her along at times when she felt lonely or discouraged.

The week before Christmas Day, 1998, Swannie was feeling rather better and asked the doctor if she could possibly spend the day with Audrey, who had invited her to Strete Lodge. When the answer was in the affirmative on the condition that she kept suitably warm and had arrangements made for transport, Swannie was delighted and immediately went into action. She had always looked after her appearance and decided that, even if she was nearly eighty-nine years old and this might be her last Christmas, she wouldn't let the side down!

Two female friends were visiting that day and they fully understood how she felt. Together they searched Swannie's wardrobe, checking out clothes that were warm enough but definitely smart. Each outfit was taken out and commented on in detail and the three ladies thoroughly enjoyed themselves. Swannie sat on a chair with a blanket wrapped cosily round her shoulders and, of course, had the final say. She was very fond of green so decided on the wool pinafore dress in a dark tartan. But what should Swannie wear with it? The light green Viyella blouse was classy and matched the skirt well, but would it be warm enough for the changeable English weather? Swannie felt that it would be quite warm enough in Strete Lodge but was sure there was a suitable scarf somewhere large enough to throw round her shoulders if it did get cooler. The two women searched again and at last found the one that Swannie had in mind—a beautiful multi-coloured shawl in cashmere that had been given to her as a present whilst in Morocco. As Swannie looked at the pretty shawl and felt the soft material memories came flooding back. Then she briskly brushed away any tears that were trying to make an uncalled for entrance and agreed that it was a very good combination of colours and would go with the pinafore dress very nicely. But where were the green shoes she always wore with that outfit? She hoped they had not been given away prematurely to the charity shop! To the relief of her friends the desired shoes were found, after which Swannie decided that the whole outfit looked rather dull for Christmas Day. She would ask Eve to get her a bright pair of clip on earrings from that nice shop in Fore Street and bring them when she came on Christmas Eve. The excitement was bringing back a little colour to Swannie's cheeks—and definitely some of her old fiery spirit. The two friends smiled at each other knowingly!

So Christmas Day 1998 came and passed by happily. Swannie often found herself reminiscing about past Christmas times, sometimes in Morocco, other times in Corsica and even the U.S.A. Some of these had been thrilling, others rather lonely, but Swannie found herself thanking God that day for the full and satisfying life she had been able to lead. There had been much heartache, many problems particularly in her work among the Berbers, but overshadowing it all such a sense of fulfilment. In the past she had often felt that little was being achieved but in later years Swannie was taking comfort from the fact that others were sure to reap where she had sown.

That Christmas Day did prove to be Swannie's last. But she was happy and had not wished to be anywhere else except where she was. She was just glad of the comfort of Strete Lodge and the company of her good friends. As Swannie had found herself admitting during the last few months, she was now beginning to feel weary.

All the travelling on earth had now been done and there was only one further journey left for her to make. Swannie continued to pray, as always, that when the time for that journey arrived she would be ready and waiting.

Chapter 18
No More Waiting!

SWANNIE'S EYES WERE FILLED WITH PAIN as she looked up at the doctor. 'It's here again...' Her voice was faint with exhaustion.

'I'll prescribe something to ease the pain but I think you are far too weak to move to hospital, Miss Swan. And I have a feeling you would really rather stay here. Am I not right?'

The doctor's voice was gentle as he took hold of the thin hand and was rewarded by a faint smile from Swannie. She closed her eyes. She was glad the doctor understood a little of how she felt but no one could possibly know just how much she longed to enter the final journey of her life. She had been at the Coleridge Nursing Home for some months now and they were very kind, but her work on earth was finished and she was just waiting.

Swannie's memory floated back to the other call she had been waiting for so desperately those many years ago; the call to tell her she would soon be on her way to Morocco. How hard those three long waiting years had been, Swannie gave a faint smile, and how impatient she always was. But then the sea journey…and then Morocco!

The white walls gleamed suddenly a brighter white. No longer the pristine walls of the nursing home but the roughly hewn stone walls of small flat-roofed houses shining in the brilliant sunshine. For a moment Swannie was back in Morocco—back with her beloved Berber friends.

Nearly forty years…faces shone clearly through the mist of her tired mind. 'Drees…and Aberbash….and Hafadowi…and all the little girls so quickly grown up and married.'

Swannie's pain was easing. She saw her mother's face, so sweet and caring. Then her father with his strong voice saying firmly, 'I'll pay…as long as you promise not to marry, Mildred!'

And she heard herself so glibly promising—but had she done the right thing? Always she had wanted to learn, above everything else at one time, and then to teach others. The dirty little face of one of the girls who had been in her class in her first teaching years came vaguely before Swannie's eyes and she smiled. Such a naughty little girl…and so charming!

She had been loved herself, Swannie knew that, and as familiar faces became clearer her eyes filled with tears. She had loved as well, very deeply. But had she not made a promise to her father and did not even the dear Berbers say that Miss Swan always kept her word?

Swannie could now vaguely hear the sound of a ship's siren in the distance and she sat up.

The words of the following poem that Swannie wrote many years before might well have echoed in her mind as she embarked on that final journey:

En-route

Going on a journey—wonderful and far;
takes the briefest second
beyond the farthest star

Don't need any baggage, haven't got to pay;
might be going next year—might be off today
Fairer than the daybreak—lighter than the air;
purified entirely,
altogether fair.

Who will come to meet me—in that other land?
The King himself will join me
and take me by the hand.

Corsica, 1971

Swannie's funeral took place in the Evangelical Church in Kingsbridge, Devon, England on Thursday, 25th March 1999. It was a time of rejoicing just as she had wanted, but there was also sadness felt for the loss of a good friend. Friends and colleagues of Swannie came from many different parts of the world to pay their respects and the church was crowded.

Quotes from tributes given by two of Swannie's good friends in Kingsbridge will perhaps help put into perspective the different facets to Swannie's character and the feelings of many of us who knew her:

We were neighbours of Swannie and she shared many of her life stories with me. John Newton's hymn always comes to my mind when I think of Swannie: 'Through many dangers, toils and snares, I have already come…' Morocco was a dangerous place most of the time Swannie was there and she was a brave and noble lady who brought a touch of love to the Berber people whom she served. We will very much miss Swannie and it has been a great privilege for me and my family to be just a small part of such an amazing life.

(Peter Hammet)

I met Swannie in 1979 at Malaga airport when she came with an American couple to meet me off the plane from London. I was just seventeen and had long permed hair and a guitar in one hand. She welcomed me gladly and became to me the incarnation of every missionary I had ever read about. I could not get enough of listening to her sometimes-hilarious advice, which ranged from being aware of the threat of danger to the importance of black olives if I were to survive in North Africa! It was a thrill for me to travel to Morocco with Swannie and meet some of the people of whom she talked so fondly. What better guide could I have than someone who had spent so many years travelling back and forth to the Berbers in the Middle Atlas? Swannie was an extraordinarily gifted lady who never pretended to be perfect but

was patient and understanding with me as a rebellious teenager. In fact, having been a bit of a rebel herself, I think she delighted in some of my escapades and the more obvious mistakes I made during first missionary experience!
(Angela Smith)

Swannie's ashes were later scattered, at her own request, under a large majestic Cedar of Lebanon tree in a forest on the Middle Atlas Mountains, very near the town of Azrou. She had spent many happy hours in this mountainous area where so many of her Berber friends lived.

A gentle rain was falling as a few Scriptures were read and a prayer lifted up to God that the impact of Swannie's ministry among the Berbers of the Middle Atlas would bring an abundance of fruit through the seed sowed so faithfully. A sudden brilliant shaft of sunlight beamed through the branches of the trees and the colleagues who had worked with her in Morocco looked up in thankfulness and praise. To them it seemed as if God were saying, 'Well done, good and faithful servant.'

How Swannie, with her artistic as well as spiritual nature, would have appreciated that scene and the sentiments expressed.

Epilogue

SWANNIE WENT OUT TO THE MISSION field of Morocco in 1941 and was there until 1969 when she was expelled along with all other Christian missionaries. She had worked alongside the people during those years but it was 1968 before she was able to make the first Berber radio broadcast in the Shilha tongue. This was sent out by Trans World Radio and what a thrill it was for Swannie to listen to the message coming through on a small transistor radio. She had a group of Berbers around her and it was the start of something special, as the Shilha tongue had not before been recognised as an official language in Morocco.

That radio work is still very much in operation. The recording is done in the Media Centre at Malaga under the auspices of Avant, now the new and more modern name given to the Gospel Missionary Union. Many changes have been made in the last few years resulting in an increase of 300% in the number of people listening and responding to the Berber radio programmes.

Previously there had been two thirty-minute programmes each week but this was increased to five fifteen-minute slots. Trans World Radio then started to air the programme at the end of their two-hour Arabic block, which meant that more people were available to listen. The format was changed in order to have a special focus for each day, consisting of bible study, questions, music, testimonies and special issues. More people are now used in the various segments of the programme and there is a local Moroccan mobile telephone number given for anyone to call with comments or questions. In order to be available for the callers another person has been added to the staff at the Malaga Media Centre. Each month there are now approximately twenty-seven new callers and 300 follow-up calls. Many of the callers are forwarded literature and some accept a personal visit from a Moroccan Christian.

These statistics were given by the director of the Malaga Media Centre and are a tribute to the work done by Swannie and other missionaries in Morocco in years past. The radio work, especially to the Berber tribes, was very dear to Swannie's heart and took up a large part of her life during the ten lonely years she spent in Corsica and travelled back and forth to Malaga for recording sessions.

As well as radio broadcasts to the Berber people, Swannie spent much time translating portions of the Bible into the Shilha dialect and was helped in both these tasks by faithful Berber believers. Swannie gave herself unselfishly to any task that would enlighten their minds and give them the opportunity of reading for themselves of the truths she held so dear. The fact that the Berber tongue is now accepted as a written language is a tribute to her hard work and patience, though Swannie often felt that she achieved very little. She did take heart from the promise given in the Bible that some would sow but others would be the reapers. This has proved to be true. There is a thriving underground Christian church in Morocco despite the persecution. Many Berber people remember

170

Swannie and speak highly of the time she spent among them; their needs were always her first consideration whether to one or two gathered outside a black Berber tent or to hundreds through the radio talks.

On Beachy Head in England Swannie gave her life into God's hands and promised she would go wherever He led. That promise was accepted and she was taken to Morocco.

We can do no better than close this biography with one of Swannie's own special and moving poems.

Quest

I cried, 'Lord only take me to the hills
And let the fresh wind blow about my hair,
Then I shall see beyond these present ills
And find a quietness there.'
He gave me hills and wind, but there I found
Not peace but my same self distressed and bound.

'A stretch of heather, Lord, and a lark's song,
A time to rest and fill my eyes with sky;
There I will grasp the truth I've sought so long
And turn it to a star to steer me by.
Yes, heathered moors were mine but nearer came
A mind undisciplined I could not tame.

'Lord, place me on a rock beside the sea
And let the strength of waters meet my soul,
Let the stern rocks teach me stability,
Then I shall learn control.'
There stared at me, beside the mocking sea,
The discord of my inconsistency.

'Enough Lord God, keep all the universe,
It is yourself, yourself alone I need!
Christ of the empty tomb this death disperse,
Oh, quicken me and feed'
He met me—little matter where we met,
I only know I keep the glory yet!

172

Printed in the United States
28495LVS00001B/175-183